Twayne's English Authors Series

EDITOR OF THIS VOLUME

Kinley E. Roby

Northeastern University

John Fowles

TEAS 292

John Fowles in the study of his Lyme Regis home, July 1976. Like his hero Daniel Martin, he collects picture postcards of Edwardian actresses. This one with the devastating eyes is Marie Studholme, the music-hall star. Photograph © by Jacob Sutton of London.

JOHN FOWLES

By ROBERT HUFFAKER

North Texas State University

TWAYNE PUBLISHERS
A DIVISION OF G. K. HALL & CO., BOSTON

Copyright © 1980 by G. K. Hall & Co.

Published in 1980 by Twayne Publishers,
A Division of G. K. Hall & Co.
All Rights Reserved

Printed on permanent/durable acid-free paper and bound
in the United States of America

First Printing

Frontispiece photo of John Fowles © by Jacob Sutton

Library of Congress Cataloging in Publication Data

Huffaker, Robert, 1936-
John Fowles.

(Twayne's English authors series; TEAS 292)
Bibliography: p. 147–61
Includes index.
1. Fowles, John, 1926-
—Criticism and interpretation.
PR6056.085Z69   823'.914   79-27531
ISBN 0-8057-6785-1

TO KEVIN, MY SON:

Follow me into these forests, and find your own paths.

Contents

About the Author

Robert Huffaker was born October 12, 1936, in Fort Worth, Texas. He grew up in Port Arthur, and received a B.A. in English and an Army commission from Texas A&M University. There he began a broadcast journalism career that was to last twelve years. After serving his term as an Army Lieutenant, he worked as a newscaster for the local television station. In 1962, he went to work for the CBS Television and Radio News affiliate in Dallas.

During the following six years in Dallas, Huffaker won an impressive number of awards for his reporting. A national award was presented in 1963 by the Radio-Television News Directors Association of America for coverage of the assassination of President Kennedy.

Since leaving his broadcast career in 1967 to earn his Ph.D., Professor Huffaker has been a productive literary scholar. He serves as Associate Editor of the well-known journal *Studies in the Novel* and as Contributing Editor of the *Modern Humanities Research Association Annual Bibliography of English Language and Literature*. Professor Huffaker has coauthored a poetry textbook and has published in such scholarly journals as *Southern Humanities Review*.

Preface

In autumn of 1970, I was fortunate enough to be seduced by John Fowles's most famous heroine. The affair, of course, was purely literary; and even at that, Miss Woodruff was hardly forward. She enticed me instead with her mysterious aloofness, a reserve I admire in her still—as I appreciate the same quality in her creator's techniques. Her courage, passion, and imagination further allured me, and I began to see kindred virtues in the novel itself. Its positive and committed power drew me to read successive Fowles novels. They rang with intelligently optimistic existentialist thought; their more aware characters could, like Sarah, act with both compassion and reason. After a decade or so of British novels with look-alike heroes, John Fowles was writing fiction beyond being classified as either establishment or antiestablishment. I mentally thanked Miss Woodruff for luring me on.

Soon I sensed a more primal magnetism in those books. All the while, Fowles had been leading me into a fictional world inhabited by birds, insects, woodland creatures—through dark foliage, across bright meadows, down foggy lanes. He was painting a living reality that spoke truths founded in simplicity, and he painted it with love. Fowles showed that the heart of reality lies in nature. His spirit is a country boy's; and since mine is too, his vision still touches me as it did then.

Now John Fowles has gained worldwide recognition as one of this century's better novelists. His most popular novel, *The French Lieutenant's Woman*, appears in nineteen languages, *The Collector* in sixteen, *The Magus* in eleven. While almost two decades of readers have delighted in Fowles's books, scholars and critics have paid increasing attention to his work. Now, as my bibliography attests, writings about Fowles and his art have begun to proliferate, and I predict that his reputation will last.

Fowles is gifted with intelligence and imagination. He is better read than most of today's writers, but his erudition has never dampened his fiction's attraction for people who enjoy a good story.

More important, Fowles accepts the responsibility that accompanies his natural gifts. He views his art seriously and loves nature more intensely than the mass of people ever do. As a result, he works for humanitarian and environmental causes, and he infuses his writing with strength and kindness born of intelligence. His own words from *Daniel Martin* express an important part of his personal and artistic credo: "No true compassion without will, no true will without compassion."

Because an author of such depth and appeal deserves notice, I intend this study to enlighten you about his life and art. I devote a chapter to each of his major books of fiction, focusing upon whatever in each is likely to strike readers as important—or, in the case of *The Magus*, as puzzling. Among my book's fundamental themes is the premise that John Fowles is a naturalist, in both his life and his writings. Another is that his art centrally concerns freedom of will and of expression, the lure of mystery and sexual longing, and conflicts that arise when man's idealism obscures his reality.

Daniel Martin, Fowles's most autobiographical and naturalistic novel, serves in my first chapter as a framework for surveying his life and naturalism. The second chapter returns to *The Magus*, the first novel Fowles conceived, and the remainder of my study discusses his other major books in the order in which he published them. Since one may best understand *The Magus* through the ideas of Karl Jung, I discuss this novel's portraying a strange application of Jungian psychoanalysis—and employing the romantic-quest motif so frequent in Fowles's stories. My next chapter sets *The Collector* against its historical background of socially conscious British novels with lower-class antiheroes, and it treats that novel as a social statement and a psychological study. The following chapter evaluates *The French Lieutenant's Woman* as centering upon the theme of evolution—in society, theology, and the novel form. And since the stories in *The Ebony Tower* share the matter of man's governing his behavior by trying to subdue his feelings, the next chapter focuses upon that common theme. My final chapter attempts to evaluate these major works individually and to assess the quality of Fowles's achievement.

I am grateful to Little, Brown & Co., W. Thomas Taylor (*Ourika*, © 1977), Ecco Press (*Poems*, © 1973), Anthony Sheil Associates Ltd, Jonathan Cape Ltd, and John Fowles for their kind permission to quote excerpts from Mr. Fowles's books. I will always be in-

Preface

debted to James Ward Lee of North Texas State University for guiding and befriending me—to John Fowles for inspiring this book, then tolerating my questions while I wrote it—and to Sarah, for tempting me on.

ROBERT HUFFAKER

North Texas State University

Chronology

1926   John Robert Fowles, son of Robert and Gladys (Richards) Fowles, born 31 March, in Leigh-on-Sea, Essex.

1939–   Specialized in French and German at Bedford School. From
1944   1940–1945, visited his parents three times a year at their wartime home in the village of Ipplepen, South Devon.

1944–   As instructor lieutenant in the Royal Marines, trained com-
1947   mando recruits in Devonshire. As part of his service, studied for six months at the University of Edinburgh.

1947–   Read French and German at New College, Oxford, where he
1950   learned to admire Flaubert especially among the French writers. Admired Sartre, Camus, and their existentialism. In 1950, received a BA degree with honors.

1950–   Taught English at the University of Poitiers. Read, among
1951   others, Gide and Giraudoux. Taught himself rudimentary Latin and began reading the Latin poets, especially Martial and Horace.

1951–   Was English master at the Anargyrios School on the Greek
1952   island of Spetsai, where he met Elizabeth Whitton. Wrote poetry, including many of his "Greek Poems." Began first draft of *The Magus* soon after departure from Greece.

1954   Married Elizabeth Whitton on 2 April.

1954–   Lived in various places in Hampstead, London. Taught
1963   English at Ashridge College for one year, then English to foreign girls for some nine years at St. Godric's College, where he became department head. Wrote *The Collector* during 1961–1962.

1963   Published *The Collector*.

1964–   Quit teaching to devote full time to writing. Moved to
1965   Highgate, London.

1964   Published *The Aristos*, a nonfiction "self portrait in ideas." Published consecutive revised editions in 1968 and 1970.

1965   Published *The Magus*, his first novel, which he had begun twelve years earlier.

1966   Moved to Underhill Farm near Lyme Regis, Dorset. In Autumn, had the vision which inspired *The French Lieutenant's Woman*.

1967–   25 January to 27 October 1967, wrote first draft of *The*
1968   *French Lieutenant's Woman*; continued revisions into 1968.

1968   Moved from the farm into Lyme Regis.

1969   Published *The French Lieutenant's Woman*, which won him the Silver Pen Award from the International Association of Poets, Playwrights, Editors, Essayists, and Novelists (1969) and the W. H. Smith and Son Literary Award (1970).

1973   Published *Poems*.

1974   Published *The Ebony Tower*, and his translation of Charles Perrault's *Cinderella*.

1975   Published *Shipwreck*, a largely pictorial account of shipwrecks in British coastal waters.

1977   Published his Translation of Claire de Durfort's *Ourika*; his new novel, *Daniel Martin*; and his revised version of *The Magus*.

1978   Published *Islands*, a nonfiction text on literature's island metaphor, and *Steep Holm*, co-authored with Rodney Legg.

1979   Published *The Tree*, nonfiction with photographs.

1980   Published *The Enigma of Stonehenge*, another nonfiction text accompanied by photographs.

CHAPTER 1

John Fowles,
Daniel Martin, *and Naturalism*

I *Fowles the Naturalist*

JOHN Fowles is one of the few writers whom one may call a lover of nature without being trite. His deep love keeps both him and his stories always near green solitudes. He and his wife Elizabeth live an unperturbed country life in Lyme Regis, the Dorset coastal resort which provided his setting for *The French Lieutenant's Woman.* The lush garden around their big eighteenth-century rococco house is the sort of private *"domaine," "*sacred combe," or *"bonne vaux"* so prominent in his fiction—and so obviously necessary to his life. Fowles's entire world view is fundamentally a biological one, though neither rigidly scientific nor effusively romantic; and such a place of retreat, green and secluded, is an essential part of it. He is a dedicated naturalist whose writings inevitably reflect his profound personal relationship to nature.

Fowles nurtures plants in his greenhouse and cares for those on his grounds, but he never considers himself owner or manager—of either plants or creatures. He simply coexists well, with vast respect and compassion for all life. Fowles has called himself a field naturalist, ornithologist, and botanist; Americans might call him an amateur biologist, but only in the sense that an amateur loves his subject instead of being compelled by professional or scholarly interest. To say that Fowles loves "nature" and the "outdoors" is accurate but not quite sufficient; biology concerns *life as it is,* and such realistic consciousness animates both Fowles and his art, both intellectually and emotionally.

Except for a year as monthly reviewer of Irish novels and short stories for *The Irish Press* in 1978, Fowles has solidly refused to review others' fiction; but he does occasionally review books on

15

various phases of natural history. He has long supported wildlife conservation and other environmental concerns, both verbally and financially as well as in the way he lives. He is chairman of the Kenneth Allsop Memorial Trust, which maintains an island nature reserve in the Bristol Channel. He pleads intelligently for people, especially Americans, to live with nature instead of persistently killing it off. Fowles does not use insecticides or herbicides in his own traditionally wild English garden, which would surprise most Americans who mow theirs and call them "yards" or "lawns." In a 1970 essay appealing for people to practice conservation, he describes his garden: "About half of it is given over to natural scrub and cover; whatever seeds there happen to be are allowed to grow—thistle, dock, fireweed—no matter how high on the blacklist they figure. . . . It harbors five or six breeding mammals, a dozen or so species of nesting birds with many more as visitors, a good variety of butterflies and moths and a generally luxuriant insect life." Fowles goes on to say, of people whom such wildness shocks, "They simply don't comprehend the rewards, the richness, the sense of a harmonious creation that such disorder and laziness bring into daily life. Nothing can annul the prior lien nature has on your property. . . . "[1]

Fowles's instinctive love of the meaning in nature's wildness gains strength from his considerable knowledge of modern biology and also from his own synthesis of traditional philosophy. His nonfiction book *The Aristos* dates such a sense of harmony-in-disorder back to the fifth century B.C. and the Greek philosopher Heraclitus' theory of balanced opposites and horizontal existence. In Heraclitean philosophy, good and evil, pain and pleasure, beauty and ugliness all work as countersupporting forces to perpetuate existence in a scheme which leaves each separate organism's fate to chance, while subjecting universal destiny to immutable natural law. In such a system, only individual beings begin and end, while existence, which one might draw as a horizontal line, continues infinitely through perpetual evolution, reaching neither perfection nor destruction. In Fowles's universe, "god" is a situation rather than a being—the situation which permits total freedom by never intervening, never suspending natural law to influence individual fates. Fowles reverses Pascal's advice and advocates that man "bet" against the existence of a judging god or an afterlife and work for the good of life in the present.

However much such a here-and-now philosophy might resemble

existentialism, and however often Fowles illuminates existential situations with his fiction, he himself values existentialism primarily as a utilitarian device rather than as a doctrine. "My philosophy of life," he writes, "rather a grand phrase for what is more intuition than anything else—is much more biological than existentialist . . . though I certainly think the latter is a useful sort of do-it-yourself kit for getting out of one or two biological dilemmas (such as that of free will). Most writing about me overlooks the fact that my major private interest in life is natural history, especially in its behaviouristic aspects. I really do take an ethologist's, or birdwatcher's, view of the human condition (also a Zen view, but that opens another road)."[2]

Fowles's interest in biological influences upon behavior is nothing like what has become known as behavioral psychology (whose jargon Fowles parodies in *The Magus*). Behaviorism—with its penchant for categorizing, explaining, predicting, and manipulating—is against everything that Fowles, with his love of mystery, stands for. Behaviorism's insistence upon scientizing humanity especially conflicts with his Zen view of life.

Fowles's Zen perspective, as he says, does open another road. But its way is quite compatible with his naturalist's view. Fowles is especially sympathetic to Zen's distrust of naming and classifying. He writes, "As soon as we have a thing named, says Zen, we start forgetting about its real nature. So labels, especially labels for common human problems, tend to become convenient excuses for letting the problems take care of themselves."[3] Fowles was drawn to Zen in the late 1950s when he developed an interest in Japanese poetry, then read Alan W. Watts's *The Way of Zen*. But he espouses its vision rather than its practice:

I am not interested in it as a philosophy or way of life; only as a way of seeing. Zen in fact confirmed discoveries I was already making in the 50s and 60s about my private relationship, *modus vivendi* so to speak, with nature; i.e., though I suppose I can call myself a fairly good orthodox field botanist, ornithologist and the rest, this quasi-scientific approach had come to seem more and more inadequate (to me) emotionally, psychically, whatever you want to call it. I think I cannot be understood properly if this attachment to nature, and to natural history, and its disciplines, from the scientific to the 'Zen' aesthetic/poetic, is not taken into account. Behaviourisms in birds, insects and plants have always fascinated me; and especially the components of hazard and mystery that any honest (and even fully scientific) observer must admit they possess. I enjoy most what I do not understand in nature, both non-human and human. In summary, just as I am not what most people would think of as a natural historian, nor am I what most would think of as a Zen enthusiast (rather precious ladies and gentlemen, in my experience). I confine it to the mind and eye, so to speak.[4]

Above all, Zen values actions which are natural, free, spontaneous, and aware. It sees reality in the fundamental elements of existence—particularly in biological truths. Its simple yet profound view takes into account the multiplicity and depths of natural mystery—and provides a natural way of knowing nature. The biological perspective central to Fowles's art is the more complete for being tempered with Zen awareness.

Fowles thinks of his own writing in terms of birth and growth, and he frequently sets a current undertaking aside for several months while working at another. He compares them sometimes to plants and trees which undergo alternating periods of dormancy and growth. Although he now writes few poems, those in his one volume show his early naturalistic simplicity. In particular, their directness suggests the Zen influence of Japanese poetry. All of his fiction reveals his obvious fondness for birds. Their calls lure his heroes into adventures of self-discovery, and they fly and sing freedom through his every story. He occasionally links particular birds to particular characters; his own surname even means "birds," and he mentions its rhyming with "owls." Butterflies and other insects and arachnids abound in his fiction; and stones, cliffs, flowers, and foliage speak a silent message. Some of his characters hear it, but because a few (notably Clegg of *The Collector* and Peter of "The Cloud") remain deaf to its reality, they behave destructively, without self-knowledge. The latter story's narrative viewpoint is even that of a hidden bird, who is apparently a person-watcher. Naturalism is inherent in the motives of Fowles's characters, who respond to the most basic of biological impulses: sexual longing; hunger for security, creativity, and approbation; anxiety over losing identity and missing opportunity; and curiosity about natural mysteries.

Fowles's novel *Daniel Martin* reveals much about the writer's special relationship with nature, and the book is more clearly naturalistic than his previous fiction has been. Like all of Fowles's protagonists, Daniel sometimes acts under the influence of various natural forces which partly determine his fate; but unlike Fowles's other books, this one plots the hero's life in an all-inclusive manner reminiscent of that in books by French naturalists such as Flaubert and Zola. Fowles presents *Daniel Martin* also in a style more naturalistic than that of his earlier stories: he employs less artifice, except for shifting tense and person. Fowles discards such devices as suspense and deliberately allows his hero so comfortable a situation as to discourage the reader's sympathy. Fowles is being determinedly real. His varied styles in previous works have always been free and spontaneous in spite of their craftsmanship, but this novel's ruminative pace, its studiedly unexciting plot, and its frequently long and chatty sentences move toward a more natural, less artificial kind of fiction. The narrator takes all the time he needs to tell his life's story, but more discussing than acting takes place in the novel. The book's only murder is unsolved, the corpse unidentified; upstairs footsteps never descend; stones are thrown by the unseen; a car outside is heard to hesitate, then drive away. Much that might have happened, does not. Fowles has kept nearly all of the little violence offstage, and his characters react to its aftermath undemonstratively. The book's sometimes Jamesian sentences—Fowles often interrupts them at considerable length with parenthetic explanations—also slow the movement of the narrative. Despite his spontaneity, Fowles is far too conscious of his craft to have written such a long, slow book without having intended to do precisely that. Throughout his writing career, critics had praised his mastery as teller of stories, manipulator of readers; chucking that advantage for a no-tricks, naturalistic novel was a choice which demanded courage, like fighting with one hand tied.

II *Fowles's Early Life*

John Fowles's boyhood kindled his lifetime love of landscapes, and his fiction has celebrated several of them near his various homes. His stories have often grown out of countrysides which have persistently tweaked his imagination. He places both *The Magus* and *The French Lieutenant's Woman* in the very settings where he lived when his mind first conceived them. Fowles's characters often move through the green country of the southern England where some of his own adventures have happened; several of them take to the dark forests he has explored in France; and Daniel Martin and his creator are in love with the same landscape they have both visited in New Mexico.

Because Fowles portrays a largely positive universe, and because he prefers foliage over bleakness as certainly as he espouses affirmation over existentialist nausea, most of his fictional settings are green and promising. But they are not all as lush as his Edenic gardens and sacred combes; he puts Nick and Alison, of *The Magus*, to bed on Mount Parnassus, then later awakens Nick in an ancient mountaintop ruin, an Aegean counterpart of the New Mexican one which so attracts Daniel Martin. Finally, he drives Dan and Jane into a Syrian wasteland to bring them together.

The one hostile and forbidding country so familiar to Fowles that its absence from his fiction becomes conspicuous is the brooding salt marshland along the Essex coast near his boyhood home in Leigh-on-Sea. Fowles has thus far failed to entice any of his characters very near that imaginatively barren land, and his own description of it suggests why:

The Essex marshlands that stand north from Shoebury Ness to Clacton form still a strange *terra incognita:* difficult to realize, on a winter's day in Dengie Flat, that London is little more than an hour's drive away. The vast God-denying skies, the endless grey horizon, the icy north-easterlies, all these belong more to the Arctic tundra of Northern Norway. The whole area is set to the key of winter—it is for the dour, the taciturn, the obstinate, the solitary musselpicker, the wild-fowler, the anachronisms in our age. I spent my boyhood very near it, and I know it well. It is not English, though it lies so close to the termite heart of England; but spiteful, anti-human, a Beckett nightmare waiting for the world to grow desolate again, and ominously in harmony with the recent grey blocks of the nuclear reactor at Bradwell. One cannot think comedy for long here; nothing will finally turn out well. [5]

That marshland stretching north from the Thames estuary is hardly less dismal now than when the young Fowles lived at its edge—or than when the medieval battle of Maldon stained its ebbtide. Though Fowles again lives near the sea, as he usually has, his characters are primarily landlubbers. They may gaze out to sea, but his only character to live on it is the thoroughly disreputable and absent French lieutenant. Fowles knows the sea's treachery; his text to *Shipwreck*, a collection of remarkable photographs, discusses wrecks and their pillaging along England's coasts—especially off Land's End, just a hundred miles, as the crow flies, west-southwest of his later boyhood's Devon combe. Except for the bright Aegean of *The Magus*, most of his fictional seas are hostile: they insulate both

lands and people—particularly his own England and his countrymen. In his mid-twenties, he wrote bitterly of his Leigh-on-Sea
birthplace in the poem "Suburban Childhood," whose sea is a
wintry death-force outside a house where pipes whine and the radio
drones "immortally / important Sunday hymns."[6] Fowles recalls his
youthful nausea at the conformism and pretense-to-respectability
which dominated Leigh-on-Sea, with its unimaginative rows of
houses.

Fowles was born into that middle-class uniformity on the last day
of March in 1926. His family lived in a typical suburban situation,
with his father, Robert J. Fowles, working in London as a tobacco
importer. Fowles never saw him read a novel. There was no literary
or artistic tradition either in the Fowles family or in the Richards
family, that of his mother, Gladys Richards Fowles. Though Robert
Fowles made his money on cigars, his absorbing personal interest
was always philosophy, and his son remembers him as being somewhat eccentric. John, who has little taste for Germany or its
literature, thinks his father's love for that country's lyric verse
slightly ironic in a man who had fought the Germans in wartime.
Although the middle-class philosopher preached admiration for the
American pragmatists, his mercantile bias repulsed his son as
completely as the thought of a department-store career depresses
his son's Victorian hero Charles Smithson. But despite rejecting
many of his father's values, Fowles recalls their friendly arguments
over philosophy. In 1961, he wrote the poem "In Chalkwell Park,"
showing the unconquerable reserve between son and aging father as
they inspect daisies and remark the lifeless weather, unable to speak
of the father's dying. Fowles and his father shared a common
interest in plants, and the boy was already taking refuge in his
special feeling for nature even in the suburban neighborhood at
Leigh-on-Sea. He has disliked crowded situations ever since, and a
skylark is the only note of hope in "Suburban Childhood," which
concludes, "I left the day they / laid a sewer through its nest."

In 1939, Fowles's parents sent him to Bedford, an exclusive
boarding school in a town outside London. Though Fowles entered
Bedford barely in his teens, he specialized for the next five years in
French and German literature. Such intensely concentrated study,
usual then for an English child, demanded that he read French and
German novels in their original languages—rigorous labor he
prizes, retrospectively: "A true parallel of my knowledge of French
and German literature at this stage would be much more that of an

American university 'major' than a high-school kid, as I was in every
other way. We lost a great deal by being hothouse-forced in this
way, but I'd continue to wish it on future novelists."[7] Bedford
School introduced Fowles to such novels as *Madame Bovary*, whose
perfection he has admired ever since coming to appreciate it later at
Oxford; the naturalism of *Daniel Martin* is partly a tribute to
Flaubert's lasting influence.

However much Fowles prefers comfortable distances, he has
never been shy, even as a child when he was finding in nature the
mystery and beauty he missed in people. His talent for pretending
developed early, in the form of skill at acting, concealing his true
thoughts and feelings so well that he wondered guiltily why he did
so. He has long since learned to enjoy being able to pretend—not
only while creating plot and dialogue but also while enduring boring
situations. "I pretended so well at boarding-school that I became
head boy," he writes of Bedford, where he rose to power in the
clique of seniors who held absolute sway over the other boys. "I was
chief of a Gestapo-like network of prefects, and each day I was both
judge and executioner of a long queue of criminals. Even then only
half of me believed in this beastly system; but it was a fortunate
experience. By the age of eighteen I had had dominion over six
hundred boys, and learnt all about power, hierarchy, and the
manipulation of law. Ever since I have had a violent hatred of
leaders, organisers, bosses: of anyone who thinks it good to get or
have arbitrary power over other people."[8]

Not all of Fowles's youthful power at Bedford was arbitrary. His
most important power as scholar and future writer was in his head,
of course, but his fellow cricketers would testify particularly to the
strength in his arm. He was such a skilled cricket bowler, along with
being a lad who must have been thought a budding leader of men,
that he was chosen captain of cricket. He has never lost his taste for
the game: he even discusses its fair play in a 1963 *Sports Illustrated*
article. A sporting sense pervades his fiction, as well. In spite of the
author's biological consciousness, with its awareness of deterministic forces, he is too morally aware to forget what is cricket and what
is not. Bedford schooled him in more than French and German
literature; unwittingly, the boarding school taught him to hate the
sort of capricious power it thrust into his grasp so early. He spent his
years at Bedford watching the older boys being graduated into duty
in World War II, and his fiction never forgets the constant threat of
tyranny.

But the Nazi blitz had one good effect. By driving Fowles's family out of the London region, the bombing brought John into Devonshire, the wooded countryside where he fell in love with nature. Leigh-on-Sea was on the front lines, and when the blitz began in 1940, his parents rented a cottage in the village of Ipplepen, South Devon. They lived in that country refuge until the war's end. Each of those five years, John spent his three annual holidays with them there, and he still thinks of that country as a pleasant retreat: "I loved Devon from the start, and the country life—lived a sort of Huck Finn existence, shot (vs. 'hunted') and fished and gained my lifelong love for natural history in general. Cities have been exile for me ever since. . . . The summer holidays lasted about two months and all kids under military age were expected to do some farm work (we even had a compulsory half-day at it each week at school). Hit-and-run raids by single planes of the type I describe in *Daniel Martin* were commonplace."[9]

Fowles was barely too young to fight in the great war himself; at only nineteen, he left Bedford School for the Royal Marines just as the battle was ending. Although a lieutenant, Fowles had little stomach for anything military, and he got himself demobilized as soon as he could. But at least his military duty kept him in his beloved Devon for two more years after his parents had returned to Leigh-on-Sea. Until 1947, Fowles spent most of his time training recruits in Devon before they entered the commandos, and he knew its wilderness well enough to teach them the ways of rocky Dartmoor, where the marines staged many of their missions. Although he does not often refer to that time, his foreword to Conan Doyle's *Hound of the Baskervilles* describes Fowles's own encounter with the archetypal death-dog in 1946 while he searched the moor's winter mists for a group of lost recruits.

III *French Influences*

As soon as he was able to get out of the Royal Marines, Fowles returned to studying literature. He entered New College, Oxford, in 1947 and spent the next three years there in what he still considers a sort of intellectual paradise. Although he read both French and German literature as specialties, the greater influence was French—hardly surprisingly, since French emphasis upon individual freedom contrasted sharply with the discipline-obsessed German mentality his own country had just finished fighting, and certain characteristics of which Fowles found in Germany's literature. Fowles is still a fine scholar in French literature, with special interest in Montaigne and the drama. In 1977, he translated Molière's *Dom Juan* and Alfred de Musset's *Lorenzaccio* for London's National Theatre, and he has published two translations of French fiction.

At New College, Fowles studied with a distinguished faculty. His tutor in French symbolist poetry was Enid Starkie, the well-known biographer of Baudelaire and Rimbaud: "She was a great character and we all thought she'd really 'lived'—swept floors in French cafés and all that. She'd sit there listening to essays I was reading with a chalk white face and a cigarette hanging out of the side of her mouth."[10] Though Fowles thought "dear old Starkie" impressive, he does not consider her an important influence: "She took no interest in me, nor I in her."[11] During Fowles's Oxford years, French existentialism made its world-wide impact, and he and fellow students cultivated a trendy admiration for Sartre and Camus. His partly autobiographical narrator of *The Magus* scoffs at the Oxford clique's aping their existentialist heroes, but Fowles's fiction still bears the stamp of that French influence. Although he firmly rejects existentialism's nausea, he espouses something of its positive and committed literary stance; and his plots are fraught with choice, his characters existentially aware—even two Victorian ones. But Fowles still insists that he and his Oxford friends misunderstood Sartre and Camus.

Fowles bases many of his plots upon variations of the medieval romantic quest, a motif which struck his imagination when he encountered it during his studies: "I was to discover later," he writes, "that one field of Old French Literature refused to subside into the oblivion I wished on the whole period once I had taken Finals. This field—'forest' would be more appropriate—was that of the Celtic romance."[12] To the title story of *The Ebony Tower*, Fowles links his own translation of Marie de France's twelfth-century romance *Eliduc*. Since such romances grew from the Celtic Britons' influence upon European culture, he considers them the ancestors of modern fiction. The Celtic romance was the major point at which the French and English literary imaginations first merged, and Fowles's own fiction exemplifies a contemporary version of a similar merger. In the epilogue to his translation of Claire de Durfort's *Ourika,* Fowles acknowledges the nineteenth-century French novel's heroine as a direct influence upon his own Sarah

Woodruff of *The French Lieutenant's Woman*, and he calls the central characters' relationship in *Ourika* "essentially a variation on the very ancient French obsession with frustrated longing and sexual irresolution, stemming out of courtly love."[13] Immediately after Oxford, Fowles drew near to the French countryside partly responsible for the haunting quality of that medieval obsession—whose imaginative tone was to influence his own writings so powerfully.

Fowles took his degree from New College in 1950—one which he, like many other Oxford graduates, never appeared in gown to claim. He went from college to France, where he spent the next year teaching English literature and language as *lecteur* at the University of Poitiers. As he seems to have done always, he was balancing his attention between natural and literary realities; he spent his free time exploring the country and continuing the voluminous reading which he has never ceased. He read Giraudoux and passed through a brief period of liking Gide, whom he no longer cares for. He taught himself rudimentary Latin and began reading the Latin poets, among whom he especially admires Martial and Horace. But, as nature has done wherever he has gone, it dominated his mental processes as much as his reading did. The French countrysides appealed to him so magnetically that he still returns to them now and then, though he seldom goes anywhere very far from his Lyme Regis home.

Three of Fowles's five stories in *The Ebony Tower* take place in rural France; both the book's title story and its translated Celtic romance happen in the forests of Brittany. The latter medieval tale especially links France to Fowles's own Devon countryside; its Breton-French knight crosses the English channel and lands at Totnes, only a few miles from Ipplepen, the village where Fowles spent his vacations from Bedford School. "The Cloud," the final story in *The Ebony Tower*, happens in a forest of Central France near where Fowles was teaching in Poitiers and close by the setting of the French novel *Le Grand Meaulnes*, which has influenced Fowles's writings more intensely than has any other single work—and indeed more strikingly than books usually affect the works of other writers.

Le Grand Meaulnes was the only book Henri Alain-Fournier ever wrote; it was published in 1913, the year before the young Frenchman went to his premature death in World War I. Fowles, who might have risked that doom himself if the next war had lasted much longer, had read the strange and haunting book a few years earlier at Oxford. Its mysterious presence brooded over him as he explored the Sologne country, where Alain-Fournier had spent his boyhood and had set the only novel destiny gave him time to write. Alain-Fournier's home village, La Chapelle-D'Angillon, near the River Cher, spans the border between two startlingly different landscapes whose vast contrast mirrors the opposition between the barren Essex and the fertile Devon of Fowles's own boyhood. West from La Chapelle-D'Angillon ranges a brooding, hostile wasteland, but eastward lie green meadows and dark woods concealing stately old châteaux, their solitary towers visible now and then above dense foliage. In those deep forests wandered Alain-Fournier's hero Meaulnes, the big boy the others called after his size and village, and throughout Fowles's pages now lie marks of his passing. Fowles, who walked those forests himself, has long told his own fascination with both Alain-Fournier's novel and his life. Partly because *Le Grand Meaulnes* intensified Fowles's first inspiration to write fiction, it affected that first book, *The Magus*, with uncommon concreteness which Fowles acknowledges: "It is one of the very few novels I have read many times and I recall a re-reading when I was struggling with the first draft of *The Magus* in the 1950's that had a very profound effect on the subsequent course of the book. I will confess that ten years later, when I was working on the final draft, I became worried that the parallels were much too obvious—and a passage that described Nicholas's reaction to *Le Grand Meaulnes* was cut out, together with other references to the lost-domaine thing."[14] The quests in both *The Magus* and *Le Grand Meaulnes* entail searching for a lost *domaine*, and like knights of the Celtic romance, both heroes seek solitude, sexual love, and freedom. Although Alain-Fournier's book is more clearly autobiographical than *The Magus*, both novels bear upon Fowles's private life and imagination.

Quite why the book has always fascinated me—as does Fournier's life—I am a little at a loss to say . . . partly because there is a link with private events in my life I do not wish to discuss. But I certainly feel a strong emotional and imaginative similarity to Fournier. Like him I had a lost countryside in my boyhood past; I am not essentially a townsman; I find it difficult to think fictionally except in terms of quest, solitude, sexuality, the mania for freedom (mania because it is the most expensive thing to 'buy') . . . and I have always particularly liked that last turn of the screw in *Le Grand Meaulnes* whereby Fournier makes Meaulnes quest on. You may care to think about that in terms of the end of *The French Lieutenant's Woman*. I did not consciously make any link, indeed it occurs to me only as I write to you now, but we are dealing with a book whose imaginative and narrative structures are burnt deep in my mind.[15]

An endless, hopeless romantic quest after an idealized woman entirely dominated both Alain-Fournier's life and his solitary novel. Before he had turned twenty, the young man had fallen obsessed with his own faraway worship of a beautiful girl he did not even know. The adolescent fixation gripped him until the war ended his life just after he had published *Le Grand Meaulnes*, partly in tribute to his peculiar fantasy, partly in trying to exorcise it. Fowles himself had such difficulty exorcising his obsession with *The Magus*, his own youthful novel inspired partly by Alain-Fournier's, that he published his revision a quarter century after beginning the book. Its plot, themes, and setting bear special kinships to *Le Grand Meaulnes* just as Fowles's imagination does to Alain-Fournier's. Fowles has written the afterword to an English translation of the novel, and his own images often recall Meaulnes gazing up at his beloved's window, taking refuge in a tunnel of greenery, and cautiously approaching a strange, seemingly deserted *domaine*. Even Daniel Martin's Jane mentions Albiococci's film of *Le Grand Meaulnes*, after Dan has told her his fascination with the idea of a lost *domaine*.

IV *Spetsai, the Greek Island*

After his year in France, Fowles moved to the dazzling Aegean, where he met both the landscape and the woman who profoundly affected both his writing and his life. He chanced upon a job teaching English to Greek boys at Anargyrios School on Spetsai, a small island north of Crete. He did not meet an all-wise millionaire there, as his protagonist Nick does on Spetsai's fictional counterpart, but he did meet his wife there, and some powerful things happened to both his creative imagination and his personal resolve. Fowles still considers Greece the world's most beautiful country, and he mentions natural mysteries on Spetsai far deeper than his imaginary ones in *The Magus*, his first fiction, which grew from his time on the island. His years in Greece, 1951 and 1952, helped make him a serious artist—and, eventually, a husband. Fowles had written some poems in France and before, but he wrote enough verse on Spetsai to comprise a separate section of his poetry volume. Soon after leaving Greece, he was at work on the first draft of *The Magus*.

Fowles has little to say of his period on Spetsai, beyond his friendship with the private school's other English master, Denys Sharrocks. Sharrocks first took Fowles to "Bourani," the villa which so impressed the novelist-elect that he later deeded it fictionally to Maurice Conchis of *The Magus*. Fowles met the real owner only briefly, and he explains that his novel's plot resembles real events on the island hardly at all. But its hero, the misguided young Oxford existentialist Fowles hints that he had been himself, is shocked into loving a real woman instead of seeking the imaginary princess—the romantic folly of Alain-Fournier and Meaulnes. On the island, Fowles met Elizabeth Whitton while she was the wife of another Anargyrios teacher; three years later, after her divorce, she and Fowles were married back in England. Although accepting real love instead of chasing the ideal is part of what *The Magus* is about, Fowles insists that his own marriage affected his novel only indirectly: "None of that had any influence oñ the genesis or plot of *The Magus* whatever. I drew on the experience in one or two very general ways, in terms of mood, guilt and so on—as one draws on all experience—but in direct ways, not at all."[16]

Just as *The Magus* breaks romantic love's illusions, its hero's ordeal also destroys his misconceptions about his own persona as poet, and Fowles gives Sharrocks credit for inspiring the latter motif by having just abandoned writing poetry before taking him to the villa:

'Bourani,' he declared wrily, was where he had on a previous visit written the last poem of his life. In some peculiar way this fused a spark in my imagination; the strangely isolated villa, its magnificent setting, the death of a friend's illusion; and as we approached the villa on its cape that first time, there came a very bizarre sound indeed for a classical landscape . . . not the august Pleyel harpsichord of my book, but something much more absurdly reminiscent of a Welsh chapel. I hope the harmonium is still there. It also gave birth to something.[17]

The uninhabited part of Spetsai inspired Fowles more urgently and deeply than he has ever been quite able to explain, but his foreword to the revised novel suggests the haunting power of the island's inspiration.

Its pine-forest silences were uncanny, unlike those I have experienced anywhere else; like an eternally blank page waiting for a note or a word.

They gave the most curious sense of timelessness and of incipient myth. In no place was it less likely that something would happen; yet somehow happening lay always poised. The *genius loci* was very similar indeed to that of Mallarmé's finest poems of the unseen flight, of words defeated before the inexpressible. I am hard put to convey the importance of this experience for me as a writer. It imbued and marked me far more profoundly than any of my more social and physical memories of the place. I already knew I was a permanent exile from many aspects of English society, but a novelist has to enter deeper exiles still.[18]

Fowles has never returned to Spetsai. Before the end of 1952, he left the island, partly to escape the depressing "Aegean Blues," as he calls the purposelessness that he wrote of in his poem "Aboulia." That verse, along with others of his Greek poems, concerns the need to escape wine-dulled stagnation—and the contagion of looking to sea for some nameless deliverance. "One has to be a very complete artist to create good work among the purest and most balanced landscapes on this planet," Fowles writes, "and especially when one knows that their only conceivable human match was met in a time beyond re-entry. The Greece of the islands is Circe still; no place for the artist-voyager to linger long, if he cares for his soul."[19] Fowles hints at circumstances which, as he puts it, "obliged me to put myself in permanent exile from Greece." He had begun to solidify his socialist political views there, as he showed in his writings—particularly the poem "At a Village Between." He was deeply concerned for the Greek peasantry, and the right-wing Greece of the early 1950s was an increasingly futile place for a liberal to speak his mind.

V *English But Not British*

Fowles returned to London late in 1952 and lived in Hampstead. He fought a gnawing sense of loss, although he still feels that he had narrowly eluded Circe. Amid his bereft feeling back in England, he faced the circumstances which provided the only basis he says *The Magus* has in his life's real events: "I had not then realized that loss is essential for the novelist, immensely fertile for his books, however painful to his private being. This unresolved sense of a lack, a missed opportunity, led me to graft certain dilemmas of a private situation in England on the memory of the island and its solitudes, which became increasingly for me the lost Eden, the *domaine sans nom* of Alain-Fournier—even Bevis's farm, perhaps."[20]

On the second day of April 1954, John Robert Fowles married Elizabeth Whitton, whose three-year-old daughter, Anna, had been born from her previous marriage. For the next decade, they lived in various places in Hampstead, where they still keep a flat. During a year of teaching English at the adult-education Ashridge College, Fowles strengthened his socialist views: "Most of the work there was to do with management/trade union courses; endless rhubarb about time-and-motion ergonomics. I took strongly to the trade union and socialist side; and haven't seen reason to change my mind since."[21] After Ashridge, Fowles spent the next nine years at St. Godric's College, a school restricted to female students. Fowles was again teaching English as a second language, this time to the foreign girls: "they were infinitely more interesting to teach than the well-to-do English misses who made up the bulk of the students there."[22] Fowles's experience at St. Godric's, along with his years of talking to Anna, helps to explain his skill at inventing the dialogue of young girls. Anna is now an art teacher, married to a talented Hungarian potter, Nick Homoky, who also teaches art. The two have a daughter named Tess. Fowles says that he tacitly dedicated the title story of The Ebony Tower to Anna and Nick, whose problems as art students helped him understand the general problems of all modern art, including literature.[23]

During 1961–1962, Fowles interrupted his work on The Magus to write The Collector, whose instant popular success the following year freed him from teaching. He quit his job at St. Godric's, although he had become department head. For the following two years, he lived in Highgate, London, with Elizabeth and Anna, who spent part of her time with her remarried father. In 1964, he published The Aristos, his nonfiction "self-portrait in ideas," which he revised consecutively in 1968 and 1970. He was also beginning to publish essays, mostly in American periodicals. In 1965, Fowles at last published The Magus, twelve years after beginning the book. The next year, he moved to the part of England he loves best.

The Fowleses settled in a derelict old farm in the dense, green southwest country not far from his boyhood Devon. Again, Fowles was living in a landscape that became one of his settings. Underhill Farm lies isolated on Ware Commons in far eastern Devonshire just a mile west of the Dorset coastal town of Lyme Regis. Fowles used that landscape, known as the "Undercliff," along with the town of Lyme, as the central setting of The French Lieutenant's Woman, the novel he began shortly after moving there. Fowles first envisioned the book's protagonist in a half-waking vision at the farm in autumn of 1966. He began writing the novel on January 25th, 1967, and finished the first draft on October 27th,[24] a nine-month gestation period. Fowles gave Underhill Farm an appropriate role in his third novel's historical setting; in the book, the old place appears as "the Dairy," its common name around Lyme. Fowles liked its solitude; he could retreat into deep woods just a hundred yards from the farmhouse. But such intense isolation, he recalls, made them wish for a few human sounds now and then. They moved from the old dairy into the town of Lyme Regis in 1968, while Fowles was still revising *The French Lieutenant's Woman*. They have lived there ever since. Although their big, comfortable house does not figure in the novel he was writing, its garden overlooks the Cobb, Lyme Harbor, where he set the book's opening scene.

The French Lieutenant's Woman became Fowles's greatest popular success soon after its publication in 1969. Readers in the United States, Germany, and Italy received the novel especially well. The British literary establishment murmured a few grudging compliments, but Fowles has become an internationally known author despite reluctance in his own England. All of his novels are widely translated. *The French Lieutenant's Woman,* long a best-seller in the United States, has appeared in nineteen languages, and *The Collector* has been adapted for the stage in several languages. Critics the world over have given Fowles more scrutiny than have those in his own country. But Fowles, whose liberal views may have drawn some of the Tory-dominated establishment's scoffing, has been too busy to care very much.

In 1973, Fowles published *Poems*, his only volume of verse; he no longer considers himself a serious poet, although his simple, direct poems show distinctively fine craft. Concentrating on writing fiction, he travels little, usually to the rural France which provided most of his settings for stories in *The Ebony Tower*. He published that collection in 1974, the same year his translation of Charles Perrault's *Cinderella* appeared. The following year, he published his brief text to the pictorial *Shipwreck*.

Fowles published three books in 1977, his record number for a single year. Early that year, W. Thomas Taylor, the Austin, Texas, publisher and bookseller who handles the sales of Fowles's manuscripts, published a limited, autographed edition of *Ourika*, a nineteenth-century French novel which Fowles translated. That rare and expensive volume contains a scholarly epilogue and an introduction in which Fowles links its black African heroine to his own socially outcast protagonist of *The French Lieutenant's Woman.* In early summer of 1977, Jonathan Cape, Fowles's British publisher, released his revised version of *The Magus;* Little, Brown, of Boston, his American publishers, delayed their edition until autumn, close behind *Daniel Martin,* the novel which had dominated his last seven years of writing. He had begun the book just after publishing *The French Lieutenant's Woman,* then had paused to write the stories of *The Ebony Tower.* In late 1978 he was to publish *Islands,* a nonfiction text which reveals more of his views on fiction.

A major concern of *Daniel Martin,* Fowles's most strongly autobiographical fiction, is reconciling the English writer to being English. His own return from Greece suggests an early resolve to come to terms with his Englishness, and *The Aristos,* his second published book, shows his determination to declare himself philosophically. Even when discussing such popular subjects as sports and gardening, his balanced and positive essays always appealed for human awareness and kindness. His 1964 essay in *Texas Quarterly* explains his allegiance to Englishness and his rejection of Britishness.

In all the personal situations that are important to me, I am English, not British; and "Britain" now seems in retrospect a slogan word that was most useful when we had a historical duty to be a powerful military nation, for whom patriotism was an essential emotional force. The heyday Briton believed that Britain was and should be stronger than any other country in the world; but the true Englishman has never willingly believed this. His further subversive ideal has always been a demi-platonic one: to live in the justest country in the world. Not the strongest.[25]

Although Fowles is one of England's better international spokesmen, he considers himself a sort of exile in his own country—not as he is an exile from Greece, however, but in a spirit of native love, though he would never be so forward as to put it quite that way himself.

For me, the best place to be in exile, in a strange sort of way, is in a town like this, in England. That's because novelists have to live in some sort of exile. I also believe that—more than any other kind of writer—they have to keep in touch with their native culture . . . linguistically, psychologically and in many other ways. If it sounds paradoxical, it feels paradoxical. I've opted out of the one country I mustn't leave. I live in England, but partly in a way one might live abroad.[26]

While Fowles admires several of his English contemporaries, especially William Golding and David Storey, he is closer kin to his forebears. He garnishes his writing with allusions to Shakespeare's works, particularly *The Tempest* and *Hamlet;* he alludes often to novels of his English predecessors, and now and then to their poems. He acknowledges the spirit of Dickens's *Great Expectations* lurking in *The Magus*, whose Lily de Seitas is a descendant of Miss Havisham. Fowles is fascinated by his own imaginative kinship to Thomas Hardy, with whose ghost he shares Dorset, naturalism, and a creative drive which Fowles considers largely oedipal.[27] In particular, the tone and themes of *The French Lieutenant's Woman* suggest those of Hardy's fiction. Fowles affectionately calls Hardy "the old man." "The shadow of Thomas Hardy, the heart of whose 'country' I can see in the distance from my workroom window, I cannot avoid. Since he and Peacock are my favorite male novelists of the nineteenth century, I don't mind the shadow. It seems best to use it."[28]

Fowles encourages people to read Thomas Love Peacock's books; he praises Peacock as England's most neglected novelist and his *Nightmare Abbey* as "the funniest satirical novel in English." He enjoys Peacock's spoofing such literary traditions as that of Shelley and the romantic poets, and he does his own spoofing with a Peacock biographer narrating "Poor Koko," a story in *The Ebony Tower*. "Peacock writes such cultivated yet natural English prose. You have to go to somebody like Gibbon for a comparison. And he has such delicious women characters. He's one of the three or four English novelists who can create great women characters."[29]

Fowles, a self-described feminist, also creates distinctive female characters, who he says dominate his males. "I see man as a kind of artifice, and woman as a kind of reality. The one is cold idea, the other is warm fact."[30] Fowles even contemplated making Conchis of *The Magus* a woman, but instead used Mrs. de Seitas as an aspect of the magician-character. He likes Virginia Woolf, George Eliot, and Jane Austen; three of his stories—*The Collector*, "The Cloud," and *Daniel Martin*—explicitly compare their females to Austen's heroine of *Emma*.

Fowles enjoys Lewis Carroll's humor, but took his wife's suggestion to delete from *The French Lieutenant's Woman* a humorous homage to Carroll. His narrator of that novel honors Henry James, briefly reminding himself not to "ape the master." As *Daniel Martin* shows, Fowles admires James's naturalism as well as his craft; he considers James America's only master novelist, ranking him with Flaubert, Tolstoy, and Joyce. He also likes the naturalism of William Dean Howells. Simplicity and realism appeal to Fowles's tastes in both fiction and poetry; although he approves those qualities in Joyce's *The Dubliners*—especially "The Dead"—he does not find such "Greekness" in *Finnegan's Wake*. He admiringly classifies Hemingway and Fitzgerald as Greek.

A major influence upon Fowles, greater than any other poet's in his own language, is that of the Northamptonshire countryman John Clare (1793–1864), one of history's few writers who have loved nature as completely as Fowles does. Clare, who wrote shortly after Keats and Shelley, had an intense relationship with nature which mirrors Fowles's in many ways; and the poet's inspiration through his eternal devotion to an unattainable feminine ideal strikingly resembles Alain-Fournier's, and consequently Fowles's. Fortunately, Fowles has controlled his own creative drive and avoided the tragedy which befell the other two writers. John Clare died in Northampton General Lunatic Asylum, having been locked away there for his last twenty-seven years. Although the uneducated farm laborer never learned consistent spelling or punctuation, his astoundingly natural verse ranks with the best in English, and it sings nature as none other has. Fowles, who considers Clare England's most neglected poet, has his own narrator-self in *Daniel Martin* mention having seen through the poet's eyes. Clare is the only other writer to whom Fowles has published a poem of his own. "John Clare," Fowles's moving tribute, defends the unschooled poet against the uncomprehending, trend-chasing urbanites who patronized him principally as a curiosity, then abandoned him to poverty and needless confinement. Clare created brilliantly apocalyptic verse as his triumph over imprisonment, associating violets with his romantic love and his boyhood. Fowles's verse wishes Clare eternally "First violets by the west field wall" and tells his kindred ghost, "You also broke the land too soon; / And made the rest seem all too late." Clare's poem "Now is Past" even anticipates Fowles's chronological frame of reference in *Daniel Martin*.

Clare's profound love for nature has endeared him to Fowles in a special way shared by only one other English writer: Richard

Jefferies, a Victorian countryman whose books celebrate nature as powerfully as Clare's poems do. Fowles holds both men in "a very special niche" in his heart: "Who was it said you could divide writers of the past into those you would bow to, those you would shake hands with and those you would throw your arms round? Those two belong in the same category, the last, for me. . . . [Jefferies] ought to be to us British what Thoreau has become for you; but isn't, and never will be, I'm afraid."[31] One of Jefferies's novels has affected Fowles's imagination almost as strikingly as Alain-Fournier's *Le Grand Meaulnes* has. *Bevis: The Story of a Boy* impressed Fowles vividly when he first read it during his childhood. Jefferies, an avid natural historian who wrote about wild England, was as kin to Fowles as John Clare was. Jefferies died in 1887, before his fortieth birthday, after producing a dozen or so nature books which epitomize Fowles's own green Englishness. *Bevis* tells of a young boy's innocent initiation amid his own farm's enchanting landscape. Jefferies's Wiltshire country is only some ninety miles from Fowles's own boyhood Devon, and Fowles has loved the story of Bevis for most of his life. "I first read it when I was 8 or 9, and reread it every year well into my teens. Though it would be absurd to look for the usual kind of literary influence, it would not surprise me in the least if it had marked me for good on a deeper level. I lived that book again and again at a very impressionable age . . . and as you will have realized, I haven't much time for the conscious theory of literary influence."[32] Describing his own hero's boyhood in *Daniel Martin*, Fowles owes much of his force to having lived Bevis's adventures vicariously even before living some of the reality he put into his own book. Bevis has rebellious spells like young Dan's, and he even meets a farm girl almost as delicious as Fowles's Nancy Reed—though not so well drawn by her author.

VI   Daniel Martin *and John Fowles*

John Fowles describes *Daniel Martin* as "fundamentally intended as a defence of the institution of humanism (for all its wants and weaknesses) and of the novel as a humanistic enterprise."[33] Fowles has taken that humanistic stand throughout his adulthood, and *Daniel Martin* supports his views by telling a fictional variation on his life. This novel of his mature years is closer to the real events of his life than is *The Magus*, his other autobiographically founded novel. *Daniel Martin* follows its protagonist's life from boyhood to

middle-age, while *The Magus* focuses upon its hero's early manhood. Writing one's life into a novel is part of what this book is
about, and, by revealing his own narrator searching for a suitable
persona behind which to disguise autobiography, Fowles hints at
the sort of narrative role he has assumed for himself. Dan's discard-
ing the random-chosen pseudonym Simon Wolfe is a fictional
version of Fowles's deciding to choose the less-artificial Daniel
Martin, who more honestly represents certain aspects of Fowles's
personal reality.

Determining Fowles's precise relationship to his narrator-self
would, of course, be impossible even for Fowles, but certain
parallels are apparent. "Bitter and repressed" Daniel is the sort of
child Fowles suggests that he was himself. They seem to have
shared a "terrible oedipal secret" in households where the fathers
were similarly monarchical; and both Fowles's religiously pragmatic
merchant father and Dan's pragmatically religious clergyman father
represent the sort of orthodoxy their sons rebelled against. Fowles
draws upon his boyhood knowledge of Devon for scenes of Dan's
youth, but the suburban Essex of Fowles's earlier childhood remains in the oblivion to which he has relegated it. He also keeps
Dan's boarding school offstage. The teenaged Fowles did the same
farm labors the novelist assigns young Danny Martin, and he often
saw the same sort of lone raiders from the Luftwaffe startle the
Devon countryside. But Fowles says that Dan's boyhood resembles
his own in general ways only: "There is very little that is specifically
autobiographical in this part of *Daniel Martin*. My Thorncombe is a
conflation of several places and families, and much is made up. Both
Daniel's father and Nancy are completely invented." Fowles also
makes clear the normal nature of young Dan's oedipality—and of his
own: "My father died about five years ago. My mother is still alive,
lives near my sister in the North of England, and dotes on her
grandchildren. As you know, in my view of artistic or artist-genesis,
the mother does play a vital role in the infancy years, but I think that
is best revealed in what he creates. The outward relationship of later
years (ours is perfectly normal, I hope) means nothing except in
cases of pathological abnormality—psychiatric cases, in short."[34]

Fowles shares some characteristics with Dan's Oxford self; they
are both interested in drama, and although Fowles did not pursue it
as Martin does, he might have. He is translating French drama for
the National Theatre in London, and, like his protagonist, he
collects postcard photographs of Edwardian actresses. His fascina-

tion with cinema is another analogue to Dan's predispositions, although Fowles distrusted Hollywood from the beginning and ran little risk of being absorbed into its world as Dan is. Nonetheless, Fowles was so interested in the filming of his first two novels that he cooperated in producing both movies, each of which disappointed him. He responded when director William Wyler asked him to Hollywood as consultant in capturing *The Collector* on film, but Wyler used the author primarily to advise Englishness in furnishing interior sets. Fowles even wrote the screenplay of *The Magus* himself and spent a fortnight in Majorca at the filming, a team effort which produced a motion picture with no redeeming qualities. The film was so bad that Woody Allen, when asked how he might relive his life, replied that he would not see it again.

Because the director persuaded good-natured Fowles to do a Hitchcock-style walk-on, Fowles speaks the ill-starred film's first line. In the first scene, the author appears as an inappropriately bearded Greek sailor, who casts a line ashore, turns to actor Michael Caine, and announces, "Phraxos." Though Fowles was somewhat embarassed by the film, he still chuckles over his role in it. "My brief career as a film star was very much a spur-of-the-moment thing, quite literally entered-upon ten minutes before the scene was shot. I suppose it passes as an in-joke, but since only Greek priests wear beards it set an inauthentic note from the beginning—one the rest of the wretched movie fully echoed. I was greatly helped, after two bad takes, by Michael Caine, who muttered, while we waited for the camera to roll again, 'The only difference between you and me is that I know I can't act.' "[35] One thing Fowles did know at the time was that he preferred writing novels to producing filmscripts. He was writing *The French Lieutenant's Woman* when he paused to fly to Majorca, and he also took time to comment on his part in the filming. "Most of the time I feel like a skeleton at the feast; this isn't what I had imagined, either in the book or in the script. Yet it is interesting to watch, on a big film production, how buttressed each key man is by the other key men; . . . I come back with a sort of relief, a re-affirmation in my faith in the novel. For all its faults, it is a statement by one person. . . . [T]here must be a virtue, in an age that is out to exterminate both the individual and the enduring, in the individual's attempt to endure by his own efforts alone."[36] *Daniel Martin*, a healthy manifestation of enduring alone, further reaffirms the faith Fowles will always have in the novel. He began writing *Daniel Martin* about the time he was getting his first motion-picture offers for *The French Lieutenant's Woman*, which defied film makers for a decade afterwards; its cinema rights sold several times before Merryl Streep was at last chosen to star. In Warner Brothers' back lot during a visit to discuss filming that cinema-shy book, Fowles walked alone and, sensing Hollywood's stagnant emptiness, even considered using the desolate place for the first scene of *Daniel Martin*. He finally opened his novel with Dan's boyhood discovering about the harvest—in John Clare's phrase, seeing nature "smile on all and shed no tears," a scene far more fundamental to Fowles's naturalistic view than his sense of Hollywood's emptiness is. But in his curt period of collaborating with the American film industry, analogous to Melville's turn at whaling, Fowles saw enough to form the nucleus of his most personal novel. Hollywood's emptinesses are as appropriate a metaphor for Fowles's modern void as the whale is for Melville's elusive deity.

Fowles has used the American film industry far more fruitfully than it has used him. He observed coveys of starlets with movie executives, then transposed them into an essay analyzing why the moguls surround themselves with starlets, as their eponyms did with harem girls. Fowles likens their obsession to the eighteenth-century preoccupation with cherubs as representatives of youth and fertility: both are man's attempts to ward off sterility and death.[37] Fowles, motivated as he is largely by attraction to the female ideal, well understands the fascination with the princess figure. In *The Magus*, his earlier protagonist-self seeks to control his obsession with the princess; in *Daniel Martin*, the principal character already possesses one and must rid himself of her. Both of these novels reaffirm Fowles's understanding that one marries not a princess but a real woman. Both also, however unconsciously, reaffirm his personal commitment to his wife, as the title story of *The Ebony Tower* appears to do by repeating the same motif: choosing the real woman.

Daniel Martin is an affirmation of several kinds. Its hero reconciles several long-standing alienations: from nature, from the woman he should have married, from his past, from his Englishness, and from artistic freedom, to mention several. By embracing these aspects of his being which he has disregarded so long, Dan is finally admitting the self-knowledge he has repressed, or else is finally resolving to *act what he knows*—a decision which echoes the Matthew Arnold excerpt Fowles borrows for his final chapter epigram in *The French Lieutenant's Woman.* In the long run, Dan's deciding is a matter of individual choice, and in that sense he confronts the sort of existential dilemma that faces many a Fowles protagonist.

But this hero is the most comfortable Sisyphus imaginable, and a hard one to make appealing and convincing. Dan's enviable situation reflects something of the ease which Fowles has enjoyed himself. Excessive physical comfort has dogged him wherever he has gone—a phenomenon which might prove uninspiring to some artists of his temperament. A great part of Dan's reconciliation in the novel is to stop feeling guilty about his own comfort, and Fowles has made his own task more difficult by allowing his character-self such an easy life. Conscious of his choice, the author lets his narrator ruminate over it himself. "How could there be anything 'tragic' in a central character who had some fictional analogue of a Jenny, a Thorncombe, a still warm window back there up the hill announcing a long-wanted reconciliation? With all his comparative freedom, money, time to think? His agreeable (despite his present grumbling) work? . . . It was as ludicrous as that: forebodings of even greater happiness—as if he were condemned to comedy in an age without it . . . at least in its old, smiling, fundamentally optimistic form."[38]

Daniel Martin, at middle age, has neglected most of what had been natural to him. He spends most of his time being a successful Hollywood screenwriter, leaving Thorncombe, the Devon farm dear to his boyhood, in the care of an elderly couple. Long divorced from Nell, his first wife, he has established friendship with his daughter Caro, who is barely younger than his starlet girl friend Jenny. In turn, Caro is romantically involved with one of Dan's old Oxford fellows, another of his generation who live easy, passive, vaguely compromised lives. Although Dan is a socialist, he finds himself writing a biographical film about Lord Kitchener, the soul of Britain's old imperialist-militarist nationalism. One revelation that helps Dan understand his own Englishness is his discovery that even the British war hawk had his own English love of nature and solitude—an island retreat in the Nile.

Chance circumstances draw Dan closer to his own green Englishness and lure him out of his lethargy, when he is reunited with old friends—among them Nell's sister Jane, with whom he had once had an *affaire.* Her dying husband, Anthony, summons Dan to reconcile the old breach of their once-close friendship, commending his widow to Dan's care, against her inclinations. The rest of the novel is about how Dan gradually decides to change Jane's inclinations. Their tour through the Middle East finally takes them to Syria's ruin of ancient Palmyra. That desolation provides the climax of several epiphanies which persistently expose the escapism behind their personal isolation. Fowles takes his protagonist from "The Orchard of the Blessed" to "The End of the World"—an effective, if only symbolic, way of setting his middle-class comfort in proper perspective.

All the while, Dan is narrating the story as his own first novel, the outgrowth of the reaffirmations which it chronicles. But his self-acceptance requires some corollary rejections, the gentlest of them given to Jenny, whose princess image he must bid good-bye. In tribute, he includes her "contributions" in his book. Dan does not hesitate about rejecting the current trends that would bar him from his novel, however. He firmly consigns them to eternal damnation. "To hell with cultural fashion; to hell with elitist guilt; to hell with existentialist nausea; and above all, to hell with the imagined that does not say, not only in, but behind the images, the real" (405). Fowles and his narrator, in accenting the positive, are eliminating the negatives that have plagued the twentieth-century novel. Such a declaration reaffirms the stance Fowles has taken from the first of his career. He has vigorously expressed his positive philosophy while demonstrating it with each successive book. Positive implications underlie every story he has written—even *The Collector*, his most dismal one.

In view of the themes in Fowles's earlier writing, the most distinctively new idea to appear in *Daniel Martin* is the suggestion that the artist might occasionally conquer time. The all-wise Herr Professor whom Dan and Jane meet cruising the Nile tells of feeling, as he concentrated upon an artifact, that he became "the river between"—that he somehow sensed the artist's living presence, beyond time. "The river between," in the words of an old tribal chief, had been the only place where men would enjoy peace. It is no wonder that the militarist Kitchener's only green retreat had been an island in the Nile. Dan increasingly feels closer to the ghosts of his past, and he recalls that the old German had described his own sensation of timelessness as feeling a ghostly presence.

The professor met his first ghost over a tomb painting, an experience reminiscent of the one in the Marabar Caves of Forster's *A Passage to India*. But Forster's ghost had been a negative one, relentlessly reducing any human sound to the same echoing omen. Forster hints that occasional positive spirits fleetingly overcome such universal negation, but Fowles suggests *only* the positive ghost. For Fowles, man's triumph over time and "the tyranny of the stupid" is his native freedom—particularly the freedom to express the depth and breadth of his own feelings. Obsessed by magnitude and quantity, pharaohs had forced their people's sensibilities into a sort of monstrosity-as-art, but human feeling had survived despite megalomania. Jane likes her cheap old beads because they have been worn by centuries of people—not buried with royalty. And Dan's task of writing the Kitchener script is just a bit like a forced celebration of a latter-day British pharaoh. His situation also echoes Fowles's medieval Italian allusion in "The Ebony Tower": while Pisanello painted nature in spite of Byzantine tyranny, Uccello spent too much of his art on lifeless military subjects. The nearer Dan approaches his decision to write his novel, the more often he verges upon such a timeless sensation as the professor has described. Several times he writes of his own strangely disembodied feeling—both as a novelist objectively viewing his own condition and as an artist beginning to share eternity with preceding ages of human creators. Like the old professor, Dan carefully expresses the mystery in nonmystical terms. He clings to his belief "that freedom—especially the freedom to know oneself, was the driving-force of human evolution; whatever else the sacrifice, it must not be of complexity of feeling, and its expression, since that was where, in social terms, the fundamental magic (or chink in the door) of mutation inside the nucleic-acid helix took place" (526). Fowles is so intent on the evolutionary magic which biologists call genetic mutation that he makes it a final epigram in *The French Lieutenant's Woman*—along with Arnold's advice about "acting what one knows," the existentially practical course which Dan, like several other enlightened Fowles characters, chooses for himself.

Two of John Clare's visionary poems reflect the sort of quest for immortality that Dan and his creator are talking about. One verse, "Invitation to Eternity," is Clare's confident beckoning for immortality through his own self-expression. The other, "Now is Past,"[39] suggests the kind of blurring of time which Fowles achieves by varying the tense and person of this novel's narrative viewpoint. By switching between the first and third person, Fowles seems to imply a greater narrative objectivity in the latter, and by alternating tenses, he gives greater immediacy to the present. But more important than the immediacy is the immortality which Fowles confers upon events by describing them in the present tense.

He began experimenting with tense in the final paragraph of "The Ebony Tower," distinguishing the protagonist's present reality from the might-have-been of his immediate past. In the same collection of stories, his translation of "Eliduc" preserves the Old French shifts into historical present, and in "The Cloud," he repeatedly alternates tense, reserving the present for actions grown timeless by becoming archetypal human ritual. But in *Daniel Martin,* Dan links his shifts of tense and person to his own particularity instead of to human universals. Dan usually reserves the present for his immutable childhood memories and for reality as it further obscures Jenny's fading image. Jenny is the ideal princess—the Jungian anima, whose unreality he sees progressively clearer as he relegates her to the past. In Thorncombe's kitchen garden, the time is now! "Like all gardeners he admires plants that show early, sense of seasons, of awakening. He thinks back again to Jenny, artifice, calls from California. Yes, the real inhabits here" (421). But as John Clare did, Fowles opposes time and invites eternity by exposing the inadequacy of traditional time distinctions and suggesting new ones less finite: he keeps his first three chapters in present tense despite their happening in three distinct pasts. Fowles has chosen to base the novel's time on his protagonist's reality, not an unusual technique in modern fiction although never before done quite this way.

In moving toward a time framed loosely by the human conscious and unconscious, Fowles is favoring nature over artifice, a powerful and consistent tendency in *Daniel Martin.* With this sort of augmented freedom, time becomes a function of the artistic sensibility in both the personal and the collective sense. Considering such Jungian theory along with Fowles's horizontal concept of existence and his feeling that evolution is a major key to the character of existence, one can see why Fowles does not permit his narrator to vary tense and person with absolute consistency. "Time has always interested me in a philosophical sense—that is, I've always found clock, or mathematical, time the least interesting way to use and experience it. And I feel rather the same about its practical expression in fiction: tense. And tense is bound up with narrating person. I doubt whether all the experiments using these two factors in *Daniel Martin* worked; but that was one reason I found it very enjoyable to write!"[40] As always, Fowles was working toward fiction based on reality, a great part of which is mystery, as he seldom allows his reader to forget for very long.

All of Fowles's naturalism supports the truth that Dan senses in Rembrandt's self-portrait: "The sad, proud old man stared eternally out of his canvas, out of the entire knowledge of his own genius and of the inadequacy of genius before human reality" (628). The matured Mr. Specula Speculans now looks at another looker—finding in those "remorseless and aloof Dutch eyes" the courage to choose and feel. "Dan began to detect it behind the surface of the painting; behind the sternness lay the declaration of the one true marriage in the mind mankind is allowed, the ultimate citadel of humanism. No true compassion without will, no true will without compassion" (629). Rembrandt's eyes seem to follow Dan now as Christ's had not, despite his youthful fears; if he is being watched, it is by eyes like the old painter's, by those of willful, compassionate seers from the past. His tribute to them will be sharing something of their vision, as Fowles confirms so often by alluding to the art of his forebears. And as he has always done with orchids, Dan will look for human reality, not merely at it. He is committed to the "WHOLE SIGHT" of the sentence he has devised to *end* his novel but with which Fowles has *begun* this book instead. It is no wonder that Jane laughs at Dan's irony about ending the novel he will never write. The greatest irony lies in that "never," because in one sense he wrote this one; in another he is writing it; in another he will write it. In still another dimension, John Fowles, "Dan's ill-concealed ghost," wrote this novel, and it is Elizabeth Fowles who laughs in her kitchen at his "flagrant Irishry."

CHAPTER 2

The Magus

I *Fowles and the Novel's Two Versions*

JOHN Fowles's hauntingly strange relationship with his first book, *The Magus*, has made the novel unique in several ways. Although Fowles began the book first, he let twelve years pass before publishing it; by the time it went to print in 1965, he had already published *The Collector* and *The Aristos*. Even after publishing *The Magus*, he remained unsatisfied with the book. He often said that he did not think it worked; to my protest that it did, he replied, "Yes, *The Magus* works as a read. But it has a number of intellectual faults, and a host of stylistic sore thumbs. It is the only book I have deliberately 'killed off' before it was truly ready. But at that time it was threatening to obsess me for years more, and it had to be exorcised."[1] Exorcizing the book that had been so germinal to his art was not easy for Fowles; in autumn of 1975, he wrote, "I have just at long last rewritten several chapters of *The Magus*, and done a general stylistic revision. I have meant to do this for many years. Some of it was flagrantly botched up, and the whole enterprise a malign triumph of content over form, or of narrative over decent standards of carpentry. I never sat down in that book without feeling its legs creak loudly and threaten to collapse."[2] In late 1977, twenty-four years after he first began *The Magus*, Fowles published the revised version—an act with little or no precedent among novelists, although the impulse to do it is not rare: Nathaniel Hawthorne destroyed as many copies of his first novel as he could retrieve, and such serial novelists as Dickens commonly altered their installments before printing them together as a book.

Fowles was right, of course. The new version of *The Magus* is better than the first, and his corrections of those stylistic and intellectual flaws that had troubled him should convince anyone who might have doubted his genius. His revisions show restraint; he has clarified the novel without eroding its mystery. Readers of the new version will have less difficulty in fathoming what goes on in the book—or in believing that it *could* go on, since Fowles has improved the odds that the improbable plot might have happened. He has also strengthened his message that events occur by chance, in a universe where man must choose freely in the absence of an intervening god. Some formerly ragged dialogue now reads true, and the hero asks new questions which most bright young men in his place would at least have considered. Sex is more explicit, plot more believable, motives less baffling, philosophy less paradoxical. Some alterations are less conspicuous: Fowles speeds his hero's travel time to Greece from five to four days, explains an avant-garde bikini, and moves vacation dreams from Germany to Switzerland. Although most of Fowles's refinements are more substantive, the revised *Magus*, fortunately, is not a different book—but it is a better one. Because the versions are essentially the same, and because most readers, particularly in America, have read the earlier one, I have used its text to evaluate Fowles's initial accomplishment—a handsome one despite its flaws—and to show what form the revision takes. The novel's positiveness distinguishes it from its contemporaries in British fiction, most of which illuminate the modern dilemma rather than envisioning a way of coping with it. Fiction's nearest approaches thus far to solving the plight of twentieth-century man instead of commiserating with him have come from such writers as Iris Murdoch and Lawrence Durrell, who suggest some comfort in man's mythological heritage, and from Saul Bellow, whose rational morality opens another positive course to modern man. Less positive contemporary writers have been trapped by the social consciousness of the Angries on the one hand or by the form consciousness of the *nouveau roman* on the other.

Much power in *The Magus* depends upon mythic suggestion like Durrell's and Murdoch's. But the power of their myth to enlighten today's man lies in taking the frame of the novel *outside* of familiar society, into the Gothic isolation of *The Unicorn*, for example, or the exotic and timeless ambience of *The Alexandria Quartet*. Fowles, too, uses a setting removed from society, and the Greek island suggests mythic timelessness. But his plot's fusion with recent history, psychology, and philosophy achieves a specific reality beyond mere mythic suggestion. In effect, Fowles brings myth into modern life with an intellectual perspective which recognizes both its mystery and its real utility to twentieth-century man. That achievement is a powerful one.

II Public Acceptance of the First Version

The novel's first version was better than some scholars and critics recognized, and it is surprising that the book was not a greater popular success. It is so pleasantly readable that it seems the sort of novel to have earned public acclaim. Although certainly no failure, the novel did not gain the acceptance that greeted *The Collector* and *The French Lieutenant's Woman*. Its magnitude and complexity may have limited its appeal; the book is so long and intricate that it may have baffled too many readers. It is a virtual maze—for the reader as well as the protagonist—so filled with false clues and blind alleys that it requires more than a passive reading. *The Maze* was one of Fowles's alternate titles for the novel, and perhaps the book is too much a labyrinth for many modern readers accustomed to the passive fictional experiences of film and television. Reactions of reviewers, some of them a bit puzzled, suggest enough about popular reaction to explain, perhaps, the first version's limited public success.

III Reviews

Most of the novel's detractors show impatience at the mysteries of the plot and the length to which Fowles extends the foolery essential to this novel. Few of the unfavorable reviewers seem to know what the book is about, and most of the favorable ones praise only its readability. Several reviews attack the novel bitterly. The *Times Literary Supplement* calls *The Magus* "a silly book and an unhealthy one,"[3] and novelist Angus Wilson suggests that Fowles wrote it for cinema. "I should hope that the next time he will use his remarkable abilities to give us pure entertainment, or better still, shed for a while his powers of exciting narration to give us a much tamer but more considered novel about human beings. Meanwhile, certain scenes . . . will make an excellent film. After all, the metaphysics will then be dropped overboard in the name of the Great Goddess Visual Art of the Cinema (or is she just a mask for the bitch Goddess Box Office?)."[4] Wilson considers the philosophical-theological questions "hardly new" elements that "merely clutter up an over-ingenious fantasy."

Another novelist-reviewer-competitor, Anthony Burgess, is little kinder: "It is an astonishing achievement, indicating obsessions in Mr. Fowles which *The Collector* merely adumbrated, but I catch, too, much of the defiance of the man who is, against all odds and with material that compression would have made more telling, determined to write a long, long, long book."[5] Burgess, who seems almost to invite a probing of his own personal obsessions through *A Clockwork Orange,* does acknowledge the book's "considerable" power, its "cerebral tone," and its "naturalistic skill," but it is surprising that Burgess, a novelist, should treat other fiction as a sort of neurotic symptom. Perhaps there is validity in his allegation of excessive length, but the pertinent question is whether the length, complexity, and mystery of *The Magus* obscure its themes.

The most penetrating adverse criticism of *The Magus* is a point made by Bill Byrom, the only reviewer to recognize the paradox in Conchis's godgame: "That a group of individuals should conspire to baffle another person until he comes to an improved sense of himself, is to put ends before means in a totalitarian fashion which the author seems to condone and enjoy. And it imperils the liberal respect for the autonomy of his characters which a novelist who hopes to invent real people must zealously cling to. Pervading the book, there is a brutality not wholly acknowledged by the author."[6] There is evidence in the novel that Fowles intends the ambivalence of cruelty and compassion in the godgame; however, his revisions clarify the paradox considerably, suggesting, perhaps, that Fowles has heeded such intelligent criticism as Byrom's.

Most of the reviews are favorable, and two early ones are more perceptive than the rest. James R. Lindroth sees three themes which appear also in *The Collector:* this century's forms of inhumanity, the nature of freedom, and the meaning of existence. Lindroth also recognizes that Nick's role in the metatheater exposes his own fantasy existence, while Conchis's flashbacks illuminate the meanings of freedom, humanity, and existence.[7] Joseph Epstein is another who sees beyond Fowles's skill as a storyteller and praises the novel's breadth: "Among other items woven seamlessly into the fabric of the novel are a study of war, a history of modern Europe, a running discussion of the viability of the novel as a literary form . . . and a thoroughgoing demonstration of various meanings of love. The book is an exceptional novel; it is a civilizing act."[8] Epstein's review comes as close as any to saying what *The Magus* really is.

Except for Lindroth and Epstein, most reviewers praise the novel principally because Fowles is a master storyteller, a genius at narration. A few resent being manipulated by such a genius, and still others suggest that both manipulation and genius simply continue too long.

For years, Fowles has protested to certain readers that he does not *believe* in any of the novel's various mystical elements— astrology, the Tarot, Rosicrucianism, and the like—and that he does not use hallucinogens. Nonetheless, a small, primarily young, following persists in trying to invest *The Magus* with some vague occult power like the esoteric appeal similar readers often find in the works of Tolkien and Hesse.[9] Although occultism is as much a part of this novel as are mythology, psychology, history, aesthetics, and sadism, Fowles places all of these in realistic perspective. Occultism, after all, confuses symbol with reality. And a very important part of what *The Magus* does is clarify that confusion. Fowles believes in natural mysteries—not cabalistic ones.

IV   *The Plot*

Nicholas Urfe is just down from Oxford, where his pretentious literary circle had imitated existentialist fictional heroes. Fleeing his own sense of meaninglessness and a cycle of sexual affairs, Nick takes a teaching job on the Greek island of Phraxos.

Abandoning Alison Kelly, an Australian expatriate with whom he has lived for a while in London, Nick assumes the mask of the lonely and free existentialist hero, the solitary poet. But the island's beauty destroys his literary pose, and the realization of his own shallowness brings him to the point of suicide.

Then he stumbles upon Bourani, the mysterious *domaine* of the Anglo-Greek millionaire Maurice Conchis, whose strange presence has been foreshadowed in Nick's London conversation with his predecessor at the school, an overbearing militarist named Mitford. Attracted by hints at the presence of an unseen girl, Nick listens to Conchis unfold his experiences as a young World War I deserter alienated from his family and sweetheart. Invited back for successive weekends, Nick finds himself the central participant in what Conchis later describes as his "meta-theatre," an elaborate drama with no audience, boundaries, or fixed development. Nick is mystified, as supposedly dead characters from Conchis's past begin to appear. He becomes obsessed with the girl who first appears as Conchis's dead sweetheart, Lily, and who then seems to be a real actress named Julie Holmes, with an identical twin, June, who occasionally joins the performance.

He writes Alison now and then and reluctantly agrees to meet her in Athens on a weekend when the "cast" is away from Bourani. Their holiday, with its climax of love on Mount Parnassus, is shattered when Nick confesses his involvement with Lily–Julie. Back on the island, Nick only begins to realize the depth of his feeling for Alison when he receives word of her suicide. Although he had begun to identify Alison to some degree with his attraction to Lily–Julie, he is now driven in desperation to Julie, who convinces him that she and her twin are genuine, and genuinely afraid of Conchis. But Conchis appears to dissolve the pretense, conceding that Nick has won Julie. The cast appear in what seem their real identities and leave Nick and Julie together at Bourani. However, Julie is apparently kidnapped, and Nick seeks her until June leads him to her in the village. Nick is at last in bed with Julie, but Conchis and his crew burst into the room, subdue Nick, anesthetize him, and abduct him. Nick awakens in a subterranean hospital room where actors whom he recognizes from previous scenes of the metatheater pose as doctor and orderlies. He is taken gagged into a large underground chamber and forced to "judge" his captors, who enter in various pagan costumes, then unmask and analyze him in psychological jargon. They release Nick and offer him the chance to take revenge by lashing Julie's naked back. He remembers the central scene of Conchis's drama—the only one authenticated by ample factual evidence. As mayor of Phraxos during the Nazi occupation, Conchis had faced the choice of either killing two captured resistance fighters to save eighty villagers or else dying along with them all. Conchis had chosen to stand beside the guerrillas and echo their cry of freedom. In the massacre that followed, Conchis miraculously survived his wounds, but Nick remembers that no one except Conchis himself has ever understood his decision; Conchis is still reputed to have collaborated with the Nazis and caused the slaughter. With the whip in his hand, Nick knows that only he will understand his decision, that his choosing nonviolence may be interpreted as forgiveness. He discards the whip.

He is handcuffed again and forced to watch a "blue" film starring Julie and Joe Harrison, the black man who has played The Beast to her Beauty earlier in the drama. When the film ends, Julie and Joe appear in a live sexual performance.

Again anesthetized, Nick awakens in a ruined mountaintop village with clothing, food, and a loaded pistol beside him: provisions for either life or death. He delights in the food, casts the pistol away, and returns to his school, only to discover that he has been dismissed. Finding even the school an arm of Conchis's power, Nick tries vainly to trace him. Later, in Athens, Nick is given a glimpse of Alison; news of her suicide has been part of the hoax.

Burning for revenge, he returns to London and discovers the real historical Lily—Lily de Seitas, a gracious widow and mother of Julie and June, who are really named Lily and Rose. She spends her Septembers with Conchis and has befriended Alison, whom the Conchis group had taken in shortly after she had left Nick in Athens. The motherly Mrs. de Seitas explains that Nick must wait for Alison. She regally subdues his rebelliousness, and he waits.

Before returning to London, Nick had visited John Leverrier, the English master who had preceded Mitford at the school on Phraxos. Leverrier, now a monk, had refused to reveal his own experiences as one of Conchis's "elect." Back in London, Nick again meets Mitford, who reveals that Conchis and Lily had humiliated him for his fascist attitudes and absconded. Now, meeting a boyish American who is to succeed him at the school, Nick keeps the secret too; he has chosen to cooperate with the "godgame," as Lily de Seitas calls it.

To avoid sexual temptation during weeks of awaiting Alison, Nick keeps company with an awkward and clownish Scottish girl named Jojo. He is trying to keep the one commandment Mrs. de Seitas has given him: "Thou shalt not commit pain." At their last meeting, she has given him a fine china plate, with the advice that he must learn to handle fragile things. Jojo, apparently anything but fragile, turns out to be vulnerable after all, and Nick hurts her despite his efforts to the contrary. Then he breaks the plate.

Finally when he and Alison reunite in Regent's Park, they wonder whether the godgame players are still watching them. The novel stops with Nick and Alison on the brink of choosing each other.

V   *Nicholas and the Nemo*

At the book's beginning, Nick is suffering from his own reaction to the facelessness of modern man, a phenomenon which Fowles treats at length in *The Aristos*. Fowles borrows the Latin *nemo* to describe man's consciousness of his own insignificance, his "nobodiness," his nonidentity: "The nemo is a man's sense of his own futility and ephemerality; of his relativity, his comparativeness; of his virtual nothingness."[10] Others have called this sense modern man's awareness of the existential void.

Fowles says that man opposes the nemo by means as diverse as religion and political assassination, but that all man's nemo-countering devices fall into two categories: "I can conform or I can conflict. If I conform to the society I live in, I will use the agreed symbols of success, the status symbols, to prove that I am really somebody" (A, 50).

Every modern antihero struggles against the nemo; but, unlike those who *conform* by opting for wealth and power, Nicholas chooses to *conflict*, in Fowles's special sense. Although many British angry antiheroes reject the establishment, they usually seek success on its terms. Like Dickens's Pip, most are after the girl and the money—and perhaps a bit of fame on the side. Though the middle-class Nick is not among the "new people" who oppose society's standards while unwittingly conforming, he is no less deluded. He learns to substitute form for meaning, style for morality—to conflict with society in the sort of shallow way Fowles describes in *The Aristos:* "I build up an elaborate unique *persona*, I defy the mass. I am the bohemian, the dandy, the outsider, the hippy" (A, 50). Fowles's nemo-antidote theory fits Nick's description of his Oxford *Les Hommes Révoltes*, who mistook their French existentialist antiheroes for realistic portrayals—and imitated them, "mistaking metaphorical descriptions of complex modes of feeling for straightforward prescriptions of behavior. We duly felt the right anguishes. Most of us, true to the eternal dandyism of Oxford, simply wanted to look different."[11] In the novel's first paragraph, Nick says he had begun to discover that he was not who he wanted to be; but seeking identity in the guise of existentialist heroes, he and his fellows had lapsed into a masque that is its own sort of conformity. Such stylish revolutionaries are as uniformly unoriginal as their contemporaries who flee the nemo to refuge in social convention. Nick assumes affected manners, a fashionable *ennui*, and the self-deluded role of poet.

He is as sightless as his conservative-militaristic father had been in substituting certain "capitalized key words" for an intellect: Discipline, Tradition, Responsibility, and the like. His father had countered the nemo through conformity: the uniform and the ideas to decorate it. In choosing the opposite course, Nick, although

better read, is hardly more intellectual than his father had been. He
and his Oxford literary circle accumulate their own key words and
even dress alike for meetings. A false identity, but at least an
identity.

VI   Un débauché de profession

Groping for identity and fleeing the nemo, Nick falls into a cycle
of unenthusiastic promiscuity. Nick's brief affairs are part of his
nonconformist persona—the quasi-literary behavior of an existentialist hero who values freedom. His consciously dramatic display of
"the solitary heart," a mechanism for jettisoning outworn conquests,
is also part of the greater self-delusion in which he patterns his
image after those of his literary-philosophical heroes. He enjoys his
sexual success and takes pride in terminating liaisons as neatly as he
begins them. Having abandoned his first teaching job partly to
escape an encumbering sexual alliance, Nick is beginning to feel one
of the questions central to the novel—how a man is to wrest control
of his destiny away from his libido: "I began to be sick of the way a
mere bodily need theatened to distort my life" (9). He has become
the professional rake (débauché) who, according to the book's first
de Sade epigram, is rarely a man to be pitied. The initiation
imposed upon Nick retrieves him from his situation; but pity is not
what he gets.

VII   The Waiting Room

The waiting-room metaphor portrays modern man's passivity, as
the nemo describes his identity crisis. Nick finally discovers meaning in the Salle D'Attente notice outside Bourani, as his smug
predecessor Mitford had not. But the battered sign links him to
Mitford, as well as to the Nazis who had brought it from some
French railway station. Fowles repeats the image more directly in
Daniel Martin: "existence as a waiting-room for a train that will
never come."[12]

In The Aristos, Fowles presents man's passive expectation as a
different metaphor—mankind aboard a raft on a boundless ocean:
"From his present dissatisfaction man reasons that there was some
catastrophic wreck in the past, before which he was happy; some
golden age, some Garden of Eden. He also reasons that somewhere
ahead lies a promised land, a land without conflict. Meanwhile, he is

miserably *en passage"* (A, 15). The waiting room, like the raft, symbolizes man's sense of expectation, the feeling that existence once was paradise and will be again. As Fowles explains, this myth of life as an emergency expedient, a state of waiting for a better state, goes deeper than religion. The waiting room is more than a convenient place to sit until Godot arrives, but religions embody ideas arising from such a feeling: the afterlife, the advent of a savior, the triumph of good over evil, a system of absolute justice and reward. But Fowles considers the afterlife a myth that, having suppressed human violence and discontentment for centuries, has now outrun its usefulness: "But the true longing of humanity is not for an afterlife; it is for the establishment of a justice here and now that will make an afterlife unnecessary. This myth was a compensatory fantasy, a psychological safety-valve for the frustrations of existential reality" (A, 31). On a religious level, the waiting room and the shipwreck metaphors justify worldly injustice. And to thoughtless but powerful leaders, they justify inhuman means.

Politically, the waiting room engenders repressive power schemes to impose certainty upon existence and destroy the hazard, the chance, that makes man thrive as well as suffer. On the political right, the waiting room vindicates fascistic inhumanities; on the left, it excuses revolutionary ones. "Socialism has its afterlife myth," Fowles writes, "not in a hypothetical other world, but in a hypothetical future of this world. Marxism and Leninism both proclaim, use and abuse the notion of perfectibility; justifying bad means by good ends" (A, 117). Man's expectation myths, both worldly and otherworldly, arise from dissatisfaction; and their irony is that they cause him to intensify his fellows' suffering by mistreating them in the here-and-now. The waiting room exonerates Nazi atrocities as well as Mitford's fascism. Should it also excuse Nick's sexual irresponsibility?

Nick's waiting room is aesthetic rather than religious or patriotic. He unconsciously believes in the attainment of the artistic ideal, the perfectability of his own existence through art. The theological zealot confuses religion with reality; the political fanatic confuses patriotism with reality; and Nick, the aesthete, confuses art with reality. Robert Scholes, discussing Nick's failure to see fiction metaphorically rather than realistically, describes his fundamental error: "he uses his misreading of literature as an excuse for mistreating life as if it were art."[13] Living and literature are so mixed in Nick's mind that his existence almost collapses when he sees his inadequacy as a poet, a failure caused by his rejecting natural reality as banal. Instead of recognizing art as part of life, he has tried without success to make it a substitute: "A person who has opted out has only his ability to express his disengagement between his existence and nothingness. Not *cogito*, but *scribo, pingo, ergo sum*" (45).[14]

VIII   *French Existentialism*

Nick's nausea is the sort which grew out of French existentialism and evolved into the form-obsessiveness of the *nouveau roman*. Fowles firmly opposes such negativism, which began with existentialists' branding ordinary life as banal and continues with French New Novel theorists' dismissing novels as invalid unless their writers contrive some previously untried form. Fowles prefers forms to be more natural than innovative, and his own fiction celebrates everyday life as wholeheartedly as anyone's has—including that of Camus, whose positive sight found meaning even in Sisyphus' eternal monotony. Fowles affirms reality over idealisms. Since he thinks neither life nor art dull, his fiction delights in even the humblest everyday aspects of existence—and such Zen appreciation of simple reality makes his art both entertaining and profound. Scholes accurately applies Fowles's positive existentialism to *The Magus*: "the kind of existentialist thought which animates the pages of this book and informs its structure is in one crucial respect quite at odds with the variety of existentialist phenomenology which aggravates the nausea of the French *nouveau roman*. For the French novelists, the banality of quotidian existence is an unquestioned first premise. Their work is to capture it in a form that will expose it. But for Fowles reality is not banal."[15]

Perhaps if Nick could have avoided the beauty of Phraxos, he might have maintained the escapist illusion of being a poet, but the island's positive reality, in effect, negates his aesthetic negation: "I began for the first time in my life to look at nature, and to regret that I knew its language as little as I knew Greek" (39). The unignorable landscape finally undermines his literary persona, forces him to confront reality, and makes him see the truth: his own art—*not reality*—is banal: "Yet in the end this unflawed natural world became intimidating. I seemed to have no place in it, I could not use it and I was not made for it. I was a townsman; and I was rootless. I rejected my own age, yet could not sink back into an older" (43). Even Nick's dreams of literary success and public recognition melt away, and his last excuse, the hackneyed school routine, fails to preserve the delusion: "Poetry had always seemed something I could turn to in need; an emergency exit, a life buoy, as well as a justification. Now I was in the sea, and the life buoy had sunk, like lead" (45). Without his artificial identity, Nick is wrecked *without* the raft, and he must either perish or be rescued.

IX   *Nick's First Choice*

Before he can be saved, Nick must choose to exist. This hazardous choice, the first real decision of his life, could as easily have been for death. Fowles powerfully understates Nick's near-suicide; only imagery suggests what changes his mind. This is one of those intensely poetic fictional passages which prove Fowles's Zen simplicity. It expresses meaning through color, shade, and the contrast of sound and silence, along with detailed reality and enough exposition of Nick's thought to guide the reader.

Fowles gives the suicide scene sensory qualities heavy with meaning. Dominant aural imagery obliquely contrasts with quietly horrible details of Nick's proceedings to end his life—how the blast will "mash" through and blow away the back of the skull, how he devises, fits, and tests the foot-and-stick triggering method. The first sound after the hammer's click during the terrible test is the wild and disembodied song of an unseen goat-girl. Fowles had earlier described the Greek landscape as a sensually provocative seductress; now the nature-girl's uninhibited voice calls Nick back to life. As if confirming his return, the next sound is the very real siren of the Athens boat. Visual imagery coincides, as the sky darkens during her song and the sea pales to a gray which contrasts with pink clouds high above the sunset's fading afterglow: "the palest yellow, then a luminous pale green, then a limpid stained glass blue, held in the sky over the mountains to the west" (48). The darkening, the gray, then the brilliance of color contrasts the quotidian and the dazzlingly beautiful. As these opposite poles of existence appear to Nicholas, he begins to realize that he is trying to create the aesthetic death with his suicide just as he had tried to create the aesthetic life with his poetry. Years later he recalls, "To write poetry and to commit suicide, apparently so contradictory,

had really been the same, attempts at escape" (49). Although the
landscape of Greece has seduced and saved him, she has only
preserved his existence. She has not redeemed its quality. It takes a
seduction of another sort to do that:

> The pattern of destiny seemed pretty clear; down and down, and down.
> But then the mysteries began. (50)

X   *The Waiting Room as Redeemer*

True, the waiting-room attitude toward life can drive man into
various religious, political, aesthetic, and sexual extremes—and, at
its worst, cause a moral paralysis that inhibits the nobility of the race
and intensifies its suffering. But this sense of incompleteness and
expectation also has its good effect on man. Fowles, with his belief
in countersupporting opposites, balances the waiting-room sense
with the existence of mystery.

The mystery that feeds man's eternal sense of expectation causes
all of his philosophical and aesthetic romanticisms. The mystery's
basic motif is the heroic quest—the archetypal adventure usually
mixed with waiting, for either bliss or mortal conflict. Sir Gawain
must wait the full seasonal cycle before meeting the Green Knight,
and Odysseus repeatedly endures periods of suspended animation.
Much romantic literature, particularly the Celtic romance, is
founded upon some variation of the motif of waiting and seeking
before consummation. Robert Scholes calls the suspenseful delays
which punctuate Fowles's fiction literary counterparts of prolonging
sexual pleasure by delaying climax.[16] Scholes calls the sexual act the
archetype of all fiction. And delay is a characteristic of the act.

Nick must wait for each new development in the mysteries that
engulf him; Alison first waits for him, then he for Alison; several
times he is left waiting while Conchis and his circle abandon the
island altogether. He waits for sexual consummation with Lily. And
finally, in the book's first version, after his final extended wait for
Alison, he sends *her* to the waiting room at Paddington Station. The
sort of waiting through which Fowles puts his characters is, however, more than suspense, more than expectation of the denouement. The Fowlesian waiting room is part of the initiation by
conscious suffering—not blind expectation. T. S. Eliot writes of
such enlightened waiting in "East Coker," one of the *Four Quar-*

tets, which include "Little Gidding," the poem whose marked passage Nicholas discovers on the shingle beach. In "East Coker," the waiting is essential to the exploration; Eliot says that faith, love, and hope are "all in the waiting."[17]

Nick has abandoned even his waiting when the mysteries rescue him from his downward spiral. The twentieth-century rake, he substitutes the *style* of the sophisticated playboy for the *meaning* missing from his life. Like the proponents of the *nouveau roman*, he seeks meaning through form rather than content, but a far more basic search redeems him.

XI   *The Quest Theme*

The quest theme, with its ancient significance as homeopathic fertility ritual,[18] is the genesis of the world's fiction. Although the quest still appears in other twentieth-century fiction, its modern version often has no end, no consummation, no return from the underworld. And, particularly among writings of the British angry young men, the hero often rejects the quest altogether, usually implying that social conditions have finally rendered the ritual meaningless. This reaction is perhaps the extreme limit of Eliot's message of sterility in "The Waste Land." But no matter how hopeless the quest or how absurd its labors, from assaulting a windmill to mucking out the Augean stables, the quest's very existence implies human aspiration. And Fowles invests his stories with hope, the promise of mystery and regeneration.

Like many a fictional quest, Nick's is linked to an unknown region. Man's search for Self often appears in literature, either metaphorically or concretely, as a search for the lost land. All roads that diverge in yellow woods, as Frost pictures it, signal the choice that will make "all the difference." Thomas Wolfe's stone, leaf, and unfound door may conceal the "lost lane end into heaven." In English literature, the powerful sense of landscape goes back to Beowulf's path across misty moors to wild wolf-slopes and windy headlands, overhanging trees shrouding the mere where Grendel lurks. And the winter lake-country landscape is as important to the story of Sir Gawain as is the Green Knight's color. The island's silent natural mystery brings Nick to his first confrontation with Self; and Fowles gives the book much of its power by describing clear water, sea caves, stones, pines, barbed-wire fence, and songs of birds set

against silence. But Fowles sets this almost romantic feeling against
a background of modern scientific thought—particularly that of Karl
G. Jung.

XII   *Jung's Analytical Psychology and the Godgame*

Having long acknowledged this novel's debt to Jung, Fowles
clarifies it even further in the revised version, which hints that
Conchis is a former associate of Jung's. Since the key to understanding the plot's plausibility is to see the godgame as Jungian
analytical psychology, the added clarity strengthens the book's
foundation in reality. Fowles considers Jung secondary only to
Alain-Fournier as an influence upon *The Magus*. [19] The work of both
men has strongly affected all of his creativity, and, although he now
discounts some of the medical validity in Jung's theories, these two
primary influences are strongest in this first novel. Jung's theories of
archetypes and the collective unconscious pervade all of Fowles's
writing, but the Jungian method is part of the action in *The Magus*.
The godgame is initiation ritual, dramatized fiction, and several
other things; but, in *reality*, the metatheater is an elaborate
psychodramatic application of Jung's psychology to Nick's individual
case. Jungian analysis aims to bring about a consciousness of one's
mental processes and to rescue modern man from his own
facelessness—a rescue which Nick needs badly.

Contemporary man's eroding identity is a major target of Jung's
theory, which attributes neurosis to a person's confusing personal
mental processes with collective ones or surrendering too much of
his behavior to dictates of the unconscious mind—particularly the
collective one. Jung's methods seek to restore the person's control of
his own behavior, insofar as he can control it, by helping him to
understand his unconscious feelings and drives, but also to appreciate their suggestions of truth, their universal beauty, and their
function in motivating him to happiness, kindness, and creativity, as
well as to sorrow, cruelty, and destructiveness. By encouraging the
awareness that the unknowable, the mysterious, does exist within
the human mind, and by allowing the individual person to retain his
faith in the beauty and efficacy of his own irrational nature, Jung's
method would bring the neurotic to harmony and creativity by
reinforcing his individuality. The theory is designed to help man
become his own magus—to exult in his own unconscious drives and

to use them for his own happiness and creativity—and for the happiness of his fellow-man.

When Nicholas becomes "elect," he is intelligent and well read, but his unconscious mental processes have come to dominate his conscious desires. His obsession with the anima image is the sort which Jung says can completely cripple a man's life. This unconscious obsession thwarts Nick's ability to exercise valid choice—to live the existentialism he is trying to practice. His relationship to literature provides one key to his problem. Confusing life with fiction, Nick interprets the symbolic acts of his literary heroes literally, not hermeneutically, as Jung realizes they must be taken. Conchis and his circle impose upon Nick therapy intended to help him understand symbol, myth, and fantasy—in his own mind as well as in art—interpretively instead of literally. That understanding of symbol is one goal of Jung's analysis: to help a person interpret the mental images which drive him. Jung writes of the symbol, "It is worthless if understood concretistically. If we understand semiotically, as Freud does, it is interesting from the scientific standpoint. But if it be understood *hermeneutically, as an actual symbol,* it provides us with the cue that we need in order to develop our life in harmony with ourselves."[20] With such guidance, Jung's theory might help existentialism work. One may be a magus figure, in effect, by manipulating the unknown, or *magic,* elements in his own mind—a process possible only after one has come to terms with reality. Jungian *realization* teaches one that real psychological mysteries may cause both sorrow and joy, beauty and ugliness, salvation and destruction, love and hate, pleasure and pain, creativity and stagnation, wisdom and folly—all the opposing forces in the scheme of what one must finally accept as real.

The theory of balancing opposites is central to Fowles's thought. In *The Aristos,* he attributes the idea to the ancient philosophy of Heraclitus, who saw reality as the coexistence of polar opposites. Although the Greek's belief in mutual benefit between antipodes appears to justify such extremes as war, Fowles advocates that man limit that kind of imbalance—a view closer to Jung's than to that of Heraclitus. Jung considers extreme reactions harmful. "Therefore we are justified in regarding all extravagance and exaggeration as a loss of equilibrium, because obviously there is absent from it the co-ordinating effect of the opposite impulse. Thus it is essential for progression, meaning a successful effort at adaptation, that impulse

and counter-impulse, the yea and the nay, should be present as an
equal and reciprocal effectiveness."[21]

Fowles, too, advocates equilibrium, particularly man's acting
compassionately and positively in a universe of counterpoles: he
rejects the notion that man is totally powerless against deterministic
forces. In *The Aristos*, Fowles suggests that man might control both
his personal relationships and his international ones under the
universal law of countersupportiveness. In *The Magus*, he suggests
through fiction the way man might achieve such balance by reconciling his conscious and unconscious mental processes.

Jung does not consider the irrational and the rational, however, to
be opposite poles. His idea of the irrational might more accurately
be described as the extrarational: a potentially creative or destructive mental process that takes place outside the rational sphere. As
Conchis demonstrates through his metatheater, the contents of the
unconscious mind are often as horrible as they may be beautiful.
Consciousness of both the horror and the beauty gives Jung's
method its efficacy: "Herein lies one of the greatest values of
psychoanalysis, namely, that it does not fear to bring to light the
incompatible contents [of the libido]. This, no doubt, would be a
thoroughly useless and even objectionable undertaking were it not
for the possibilities of a renewal of life that lie in the repressed
contents."[22] By presenting Nick with aesthetic, mythic, and historical images from the human unconscious, the godgame applies Jung's
"individuation" process.

Jungian individuation aims to give a person awareness and courage to behave as an individual rather than as the kind of imitator
Nick has become. Jung calls such self-deluding poses as Nick's
literary persona collective behavior which only appears individual.
The Latin *persona* was originally an actor's mask; unmasking so
often, the godgame players encourage Nick to do the same. Individuation also seeks to replace unconscious behavior with conscious
action.[23]

As therapist, Conchis maintains proper emotional distance from
his patient, but the mysterious aloofness of his magus pose is
particularly compatible with tactics of Jung, who recognizes that
primitive sorcerers explored the unconscious to manipulate its
powers.[24] As conjurer of the unconscious, the psychoanalyst pursues similar goals, and Jung, who occasionally calls the analyst a
"medical exorcist," supports his use of mystery: "Even the so-called
highly scientific suggestion-therapy employs the wares of the

medicine-man and the exorcising Schaman. And please, why should it not?"[25] Jung even specifies the kind of flexibility Conchis uses: "One might almost say practice must first and foremost submit to the laws of opportunism."[26] The godgame selects its patient by hazard, then improvises his treatment within a loosely formulated plan.

Jungian individuation's dredging up unconscious images to flood the consciousness increases one's awareness of symbol in a "constructive" way unlike Freud's "reductive" (literally leading-back) method, which seeks to dominate unconscious drives by exposing their origin. Jung considers his own way more sophisticating and civilizing, since understanding symbol can dispel nameless fears which haunted the primitive mind: "Mankind has been freed from these senseless anxieties by the continually progressive symbol-formation which leads to culture. The regression to nature must therefore necessarily be followed by a synthetic building up of the symbol."[27]

Contrary to Nick's complacent, Oxford-bred sophistication, he is not civilized enough to understand the symbolic messages of literature or of his own unconscious mind. Just as he must learn to interpret literature symbolically, he must also learn to regard symbols hermeneutically instead of accepting them as efficacious in themselves. This paramount difference is what separates the godgame from the occult. Although *The Magus* depends upon symbol, including the cabalistic symbolism which accompanies various phases of Nicholas's underground ritual initiation, it would be a mistake to conclude that Fowles is hinting at some sort of occult and esoteric solution to the dilemma of man—or, for that matter, any solution within the identifiable framework of any existing religion, whether pagan or Christian. Although the message of the novel is, in one important way, theological and moral, its theology and morality cannot be confined to any doctrine, either religious or occult.

As the image of magician-analyst applies Jung's method, so does the use of hermetic symbols. The metatheater's symbol, ritual, myth, sex, art, and cruelty—and its parables of Nygaard, de Deukans, and Foulkes—all have some conscious relationship to both Nick and the entire race of man. And in keeping with Jung's method, they are also linked to the irrational—to the unconscious mind. The godgame's symbols can guide Nick, unless he should mistake them for reality; that is why Conchis continually exposes the masque—and why Fowles, in such works as *Daniel Martin, The French Lieutenant's Woman*, and *The Ebony Tower*, often exposes the pretenses of his own narrative.

XIII   *Ritual, Symbol, and Myth in the Godgame*

Sets of codified symbols in the novel have confused readers somewhat, especially those who read only the book's first version. The Tarot elements, for example, have sent some on the "wild goose chase through the cards" that Eliot accused certain critics of pursuing in the case of "The Waste Land." Fowles denies that he intended the novel's chapters to number the same as the cards in the Tarot pack, terming the correspondence pure coincidence. And only a few other parallels are obvious: Conchis as Magus, Nick as Fool and Hanged Man, Mrs. de Seitas as Empress, and Lily, Rose, and Alison as variations of High Priestess. Marvin Magalaner mentions some of these parallels in his essay on the book's Tarot symbols (and links the name de Seitas to medieval Latin *seitas*, "self"), but he wisely rejects too much precise comparison and compliments the book's restraint in such matters as "one of the marks of the serious novel."[28] There are other correspondences, but none is absolute. The rose and cross of the final ritual suggest Rosicrucianism; Lily and Rose correspond nominally to flower symbols on the Tarot Magus card; and the mandala appears universally. Most of the Tarot symbols as revised by Waite's Hermetic Order of the Golden Dawn match those in alchemy, the Hebrew Cabala, Masonic ritual, and both ancient and modern religions.

One parallel in ancient religion is the resemblance of the godgame to the Greek Eleusinian Mysteries, which took place centuries before at Eleusis, a short distance from the fictional location of Phraxos. In these rites at the temple of Demeter, Persephone-Kore was summoned with a bell, as are Nick and Lily; light effects were important, as they are in Conchis's metatheater; the initiates participated in boundless dramas *(dromena)* in search of Persephone, as Nick seeks Julie; the Hierophant showed the initiates sacred objects *(deiknymena)* and taught them with sacred words *(legomena)*, as Conchis displays artifacts and tells his story; the Hierophant raised his arms in a manner reminiscent of Conchis's and Lily de Seitas's Ka gesture; there was purification by water, like Nick's various baptisms in the Aegean; the initiates were specially costumed with one shoulder left bare, like Nick's dress for the underground "trial"; vulgar taunts were hurled at initiates, corresponding to the degradations Nick suffers; all initiates kept the ritual absolutely secret after the mysteries, as do Nick and Leverrier; and the ritual was absolutely ended at their departure, with no further requirement of initiates beyond everyday living—just as the godgame finally leaves Nick and Alison on their own.[29]

Such resemblance among symbols supports Jung's theory that archetypes in the collective unconscious are timeless and universal. Jung shows how alchemical methods resembled his own, and how hermetic training tried to induce the same self-awareness that psychoanalysis does. He also explains how his motives and methods are like those of Zen initiation. In his foreword to Suzuki's *Introduction to Zen Buddhism*, Jung likens Zen *satori* to his own individuation process—and Zen's master-pupil relationship to one between analyst and patient.[30]

The godgame applies Jungian method through an elaborate series of fictions—some as bafflingly simple as anecdotes with which Zen masters teach their pupils. Fowles calls his own view of life a Zen one because of its simple and unshakable appreciation of all nature,[31] and Jung says that the "only true answer" to the anecdotes comes from "Nature herself." That answer, of course, implies life's key secret: honestly loving even nature's simpler forms, knowing that "there is no truth beyond magic," as Fowles's anecdote of the Prince and the Magician teaches.

Like Jung's methods, various ancient rites confront an initiate with so many symbols that he becomes aware of what is in his unconscious mind. The godgame has already begun to fill Nick's consciousness with symbol even before he meets Conchis: Mitford's warning, tales in the *taverna*, marked poems at Moutsa, a breath of perfume, the trisyllabic bell. At Bourani, symbols come to Nick in various forms: Telemann on the harpsichord, the priapus statue, the fallen glove, even casual remarks from Conchis. He mentions skull and snout as Albanian meanings of Bourani and Moutsa, though he avoids the latter's phallic suggestions.[32] After showing Nick supposedly original art, Conchis animates the symbol as a novelist might place fiction with known history to make it credible and immediate; his friend Modigliani had painted his mother. While insisting that the novel is as dead as alchemy, Conchis is using methods of both, scoffing at Forster's "only connect" while doing it himself.

He carefully distributes erotic symbols that range from myth to

pornography. Such extremes as the chaste Lily and the sullied
Foulkes set the mood for the metatheater's conflicting the Apollo-
nian and Dionysian poles of the unconscious, the battle of reason
and irrational. Conchis first presents unreason in the form of human
madness that had thought the Great War noble and patriotic—
irrationality as deadly as the suicide lottery he offers Nick. The
young Conchis, perhaps fictionally, had found that all people must
confront the irrational in their fellow-man. Unreason not only drives
a soldier to his death with the blindness of a Captain Montague but
also alienates a reasoning deserter from family and sweetheart.
Conchis presents his fiction on both levels: the rational, in which he
speaks for moral responsibility in spite of man's unreason—and the
irrational's aesthetic side, literature, art, music, and drama.

Conchis demonstrates that various ideals arising from the unconscious cannot be trusted, despite their attractiveness. Luring the
octopus with a cloth, he shows how it dies in pursuit of the
ideal—not the *real*; he exposes the century's major wars as idealistic
follies; and, staging the death of a satyr chasing a nymph, he
discloses another peril in man's quest for the ideal. Devotion to
political ideals may spawn wars and enslavement, but foolish pursuit
of the sexual ideal can destroy man in other ways.

Jung terms the male's mental concept of the sexual ideal the
"anima"—the figure of perfect femininity, eternal object of the
masculine quest. The anima is the female archetype within the male
psyche, just as the "animus" is the male archetype in a woman's
mind. Like most collective mental images, these ideals may be
constructive in proper perspective, or they may be destructive if
mistaken for reality. The anima, as Jung explains, is never a
maternal figure but takes forms ranging from seductress to virgin
goddess: "She is companion and friend, in her favourable aspect; in
her unfavourable role, she is the courtesan."[33] Alison might be what
Jung calls the "authentic" stage of Nick's anima image, but Nick
ignores the real woman in pursuit of the ideal—a folly typifying
modern man's Don Juanism, which, like power politics, is an
obsession impeding human goodness.

On another level, the octopus parable shows female vulnerability
to male seduction. If Nick wishes, he may spend his part of eternity
luring Aphrodite to her ruin—and he will have accomplished nothing remarkable. In Fowles's poem "Anadyomene" (*Poems*), the
octopus is more clearly the ruined woman. But Aphrodite the
seduced is seductress as well, and Lily plays a convincing Circe.

Nick's thread from her dress resembles the rag that entices the octopus: both are surrogates for the ideal. And unattainable ideals are poor substitutes for reality.

XIV *The Disintoxication*

The so-called disintoxication at the godgame's latter stages forces Nick to distinguish between real and ideal. He must be liberated from obsession with the anima figure in the form of Lily–Julie. Returning Nick to reality is one function of the vivid sexual message that Julie is not what he has fancied her. The disintoxication may also prevent an effect which Jung calls *Gottähnlichkeit,* a state of "god-almightiness" in which therapeutic use of symbols deludes the patient into an unwarranted sense of power and knowledge. [34] Conchis and his circle have carefully accompanied the symbol buildup with clearly reasonable guidance, to keep Nick's reality in perspective and his god-almightiness at bay.

The disintoxication applies Jung's method also in other ways, since Jung advocates leading the patient to understand the therapy so well that he may continue it himself after analysis. Conchis has repeatedly revealed his own pretenses, and the self-exposure in the underground trial clarifies at least two key points in Jung's theory. The unmasking suggests that, beneath the masks, history's conjurers of the supernatural all practiced mental science—and that images of witches, wizards, shamans, and corn dolls in the collective unconscious are instruments of mental suggestion instead of forces to be feared or worshipped. The downright funny parody of psychological jargon after the unmasking reduces Nick's psychological anguish to its basic causes. Jung considers such Freudian method valid in destroying illusion; in Nick's case, it can hardly miss, since he is literally a captive audience.

XV *Pain and Morality*

The novel's first version left one wondering how *moral* it is for Conchis and his *aristoi*, with their "rich, intelligent lives," to impose such harsh treatment without the patient's consent. The revision treats Nick with a bit more kindness and further reduces the paradox by clarifying the godgame's ends and means; Mrs. de Seitas's commandment even changes from "Thou shalt not commit pain" to "Thou shalt not inflict unnecessary pain." Causing pain is a central issue of the novel, whose first two de Sade epigrams suggest a link between Nick's former playboy behavior and the kind of sex torture the Nazis committed. The third de Sade passage pleads for a philosophy which could guide man's behavior by teaching him to understand his own drives: precisely what the Jungian treatment intends. If the individuation process has succeeded, Nick will become a sort of magus by using his own unconscious drives instead of being their slave.

Conscious, moral behavior of this sort can overcome the indirection of modern man, who no longer feels guided by a ruling god. Various fascisms and revolutionisms of the century have agonized humankind by trying to replace moribund religious commandments with armed force. For some years, Western civilization's only opposition to such insane cruelty lay in its faith in democratic institutions. French existentialism seemed to offer a philosophically sound morality, but its mandate often frightened the individual as much as his awareness of God's nonexistence. The message of Sartre and Camus is that man be guided only by the Self—investing personal choice with godlike significance. But for the vast majority, the new freedom was useless without self-awareness.

The Magus presents a coherent answer: knowing one's freedom as the existentialists did, while guiding that freedom by knowing oneself. Such conscious morality transcends simplistic "situation ethics" and "the new morality," which distill down to doing what feels good and hurts no one else. That sort of nemo morality had stifled Nick's creativity and abandoned him to purposelessness. Now, unintentionally hurting even clownish Jojo,[35] then breaking Mrs. de Seitas's plate, Nick realizes how difficult it is to avoid inflicting pain—and breaking commandments. His moral awareness must supersede commandment.

Part of Nick's folly had been obeying a hypothetical, knowable god, albeit a literary one: "I had acted as if a third person was watching and listening and giving me marks for good or bad behavior—a god like a novelist, to whom I turned, like a character with the power to please, the sensitivity to feel slighted, the ability to adapt himself to whatever he believed the novelist-god wanted" (467). By assuming the function of novelist-god, among other god-like roles, Conchis has shown Nick what it would really have been like to be judged by an intervening deity. By absconding, he teaches him what freedom really is.

Since God's nonintervention gives man absolute freedom, then man's freedom becomes proof of God. As Conchis had told Nicholas, the terrible spirit of self in the tortured guerrilla, as much a criminal as a defender of freedom, had shown him the meaning of the word *eleutheria*, and of God:

He was the immalleable, the essence, the beyond reason, beyond logic, beyond civilization, beyond history. He was not God, because there is no God we can know. But he was a proof that there is a God that we can never know. He was the final right to deny. To be free to choose. He, or what manifested itself through him, even included the insane Wimmel, the despicable German and Austrian troops. He was every freedom, from the very worst to the very best. The freedom to desert on the battlefield of Neuve Chapelle. The freedom to confront a primitive God at Seidevarre. The freedom to disembowel peasant girls and castrate with wire cutters. I mean he was something that passed beyond morality but sprang out of the very essence of things—that comprehended all, the freedom to do all, and stood against only one thing—the prohibition not to do all. (376–77)

The one prohibition which the godgame leaves Nicholas seems almost intended to be broken, to show him that his moral responsibility goes beyond a doctrine, even beyond rational processes Conchis tells Nick that his choice to die with the guerrillas had been an action *beyond reason*: "My reason had repeatedly told me I was wrong, Yet my total being still tells me I was right" (377).

At last, beyond reason, Nick sees the commandment not as a simple prohibition but as something he must choose, as he must choose Alison: "I knew that I *had* to choose it, every day, even though I went on failing to keep it, had every day to choose it, every day to try to live by it. And I knew that it was all bound up with Alison; with choosing Alison, and having to go on choosing her every day" (566). Ultimately, the freedom of choice connected with Alison and with the single commandment is a reason for Nick's slapping Alison when the novel's original version reunites them in Regent's Park. Nick must resolve his anger at the godgame's violating his human dignity, and when he thinks that the perpetrators of that indignity are watching from among the stone gods on the Regency facade, his desire for revenge against them finally merges with his choosing Alison. The slap may show her that he is no longer wearing a mask but is honestly and *beyond reason* acting upon his anger, defying the godgame crew he supposes to be watching; the slap is also his way of choosing Alison, while leaving her free to choose. Nick assures her of future uncertainty in their relationship yet shows his own readiness to take the risk: "*Pain*. We stared wildly at each other for a moment. Not in love. No name, no name, but unable to wear masks" (581).

XVI   *The Absconding*

The slap may have defied the godgame, but Nick realizes that the stone gods on the facade, like mythical creatures in *L'astrée*, are not real: "It was logical, the characteristic and perfect final touch to the godgame. They had absconded. . . . How could they be so cold? So inhuman? So incurious? So load the dice and yet leave the game? And if I wasn't sure?" (581). If he were not sure, Nick might be waiting miserably for the self-appointed gods' next move. Fowles writes in *The Aristos:* "A god who revealed his will, who 'heard' us, who answered our prayers, who was propitiable, the kind of god simple people like to imagine would be desirable: such a god would destroy all our hazard, all our purpose and all our happiness." Fowles goes on, in the section of that book entitled "The Godgame," to assert that the divine way of governing all fairly and equally would be not to govern at all, "a situation in which the governed must govern themselves. If there had been a creator, his second act would have been to disappear" (A, 18–19). Nick, no longer watched by his novelist-god, must act responsibly on his own. He alone is his own judge, as Conchis had been when he faced the Nazi machine guns.

The godgame has taught Nick to live life instead of questioning its purpose. The wreck-and-raft assumption, the waiting-room attitude toward existence, assumes that god will eventually solve all mystery and end all imperfection. No longer deluded by such great expectations of the future, Nick is free to act constructively in the present. Fowles considers reality's mystery the best possible situation for man "because everywhere, below the surface, we do not know; we shall never know why; we shall never know tomorrow; we shall never know a god or if there is a god; we shall never even know ourselves. This mysterious wall around our world and our perception of it is not there to frustrate us but to train us back to the now, to life, to our time being" (A, 20). Conchis had refused to explain what it all meant even while acting various roles of god. By replying, "In this respect treat me as if I did not exist" (167), he had suggested that Nick consider the question moot outside the godgame as well.

The masque's repeated emphasis of death has taught Nick to

appreciate life. After his release, he no longer thinks the quotidian banal as he had while affecting existentialist nausea. Awakening in a dead city, he savors food, rejects suicide, and later slips his last money to sleeping peasants on the Phraxos boat. His underground ordeal and Alison's feigned suicide, their symbolic deaths, have reunited them at last on All Hallow's Eve, an autumn merging of Eros and Thanatos, with "the stinging smell of burning leaves." Death is too certain and life too short for Nick to waste his existence on unanswerable questions and impossible ideals. Alison is the reality he had almost lost while seeking the unreal, as Alain-Fournier's Meaulnes had lost the real woman in his quest for the perfect one. At the last of both of the novel's versions, Fowles keeps the story alive by withholding a conclusive ending, but his final Latin epilogue suggests his own wish: "May one who has never loved, love tomorrow; and may one who has loved, love tomorrow."

The Nicholas who narrates the story is hardly the callow young man just down from Oxford. The mature Nicholas shows that he can now interpret his own life while narrating it, even seeing the significance of Conchis' symbols. As he describes how he had tried to absorb the fact of Alison's death before the end of the metatheater, he shows that he understands Conchis' central parable:

By this sinister elision, this slipping from true remorse, the belief that the suffering we have precipitated ought to ennoble *us*, or at least make us less ignoble from then on, to disguised self-forgiveness, the belief that suffering in some way ennobles *life*, so that the precipitation of pain comes, by such a cockeyed algebra, to equal the ennoblement, or at any rate the enrichment, of life, by this characteristically twentieth-century retreat from content into form, from meaning into appearance, from ethics into aesthetics, from *aqua* into *unda*, I dulled the pain of that accusing death. (347)

By accepting reality, Nick has learned the lesson in the story of the Prince and the Magician, which he finds in Bourani's underground bunker, Earth. The prince is like modern man who believes (as his father, or Reason, tells him) that no illusions (islands or princesses) exist. But when he *sees* such things, he suspects (as the island magician, or the Irrational, tells him) that *all* is illusory, even his father (his rational powers). When the father confesses that he *is* a magician (that reality is partly a product of illusion), the prince finally decides to accept both the commonplace and the fantastic— thus becoming a magician himself. Accepting that there is no truth beyond magic is accepting that there is no truth beyond the hazard and mystery of reality. Nick, like the prince, accepts two-dimensional reality: both conscious and unconscious perceptions. Like a magician, he can now *use* both levels of his own mind.

XVII   *Imagery and Allusion*

While Conchis scoffs at "Only Connect" while following the advice, Fowles himself is connecting his themes with image and allusion. Birds play an important part in this book as they do in virtually every one Fowles has written. He dearly loves birds, and their flight and calls suggest freedom, awareness, and beauty throughout his works. As early as the first chapter, Nick has a "strange exuberant sense of taking wing"; against the silence of Phraxos, birds call him to seek self-awareness and freedom. The young Conchis trying to notate birdsong epitomizes the attempt to scientize beauty and liberty. In the Edenic Parnassus scene, "some bird like a lark" sings above them in the silence. Henrik Nygaard gazes out of his madness at the sound of ducks in the night sky. A flight of gray pigeons and a blackbird singing out of season are "fragments of freedom" in the novel's last lines.

A prominent function of the birdsong is its call to self-knowledge. In Fowles's poem "Apollo," which recreates in a distinctively Zen way the scene at Moutsa—its stones, pines, and silent water—the final lines, set against the silence, are "shrike screams / I come." A bird first calls Nick to approach Bourani: "Some warbler in the thickest of the bushes reeled out a resonant, stuttering song. It must have been singing only a few feet from me, with a sobbing intensity, like a nightingale, but much more brokenly. A warning or a luring bird? I couldn't decide, though it was difficult not to think of it as meaningful. It scolded, fluted, screeched, jugjugged, entranced" (56). Nick has already been summoned back from suicide by the wild, birdlike song of an unseen girl. Now, the hidden bird calls him to further self-exploration, like the one that gives the call to exploration in the first of Eliot's *Four Quartets,* the last of which, "Little Gidding," is marked in the book Nick finds at Moutsa. Imagery in "Burnt Norton," the first of the quartets, is very like Fowles's: Eliot's thrush calls in response to silent music in the foliage, inviting the explorer to find reality around the corner and through the first gate—Nick's very path to Bourani.[36]

A later scene in the book's first version echoes another of the marked passages, Pound's "Canto XLVII." The images surround the

beginning of Conchis's life story. "Away at the far feet of the
mountains there was a thin dust of ruby lights in the deepest
shadows. I didn't know whether he meant simply, look; or that the
lamps were in some way symbolic of the elect" (94). The scene
recalls Pound's imagery following the canto's call to seek awareness
even with the ignorance of "drugged beasts." Pound links his
picture of red lamps at the cliff's base to the shed blood of Tamuz–
Adonis, whose descent to the underworld suggests the depths to
which Nick must go in his quest for self-knowledge. [37]

Nick announces some of the novel's literary allusions himself, for
example the Shakespearean parallels in which he takes the role of
both Ferdinand, under Prospero's spell, and Malvolio, the dupe of
Twelfth Night. Just before breaking Nick's illusion in the novel's
first version, Julie goes through a series of tableaux, the first of
which recalls "King Cophetua and the Beggar Maid," an English
ballad of a misogynist king who marries a peasant girl he spies
through his palace window, an echo of de Deukans's hearing the
girl's laugh through his window. Although no beggar, Alison is
"coarse salt," and her language, sexual experience, and Australian
background make her a misfit to Nick's Oxford pretentiousness. [38]

XVIII   The Magus *and Today's Fiction*

In this era of antiheroes who lack power to act, *The Magus* is a
positive change: Fowles restores Nick to action. In judging the
book's impact among its contemporaries, we must ask whether the
restoration holds any optimism for the rest of twentieth-century
man. I think it does. Although we cannot all be saved by millionaire
psychiatrists, we can read Nick's telling of his initiation—and including in it Conchis's telling his. *Printed* fiction initiates us, less
expensively and forcibly than the godgame does Nick; but if we
repeat Nick's mistake and take it too literally, we are back where
much of today's fiction already was—with the passive contemporary
hero in his personal waiting room.

Before Nick's reunion with Alison, he is left in the waiting-room
situation that faces other antiheroes, but Fowles frees him from that
cell and gives him the power to act upon his feelings. Other
antiheroes have stayed waiting at novel's end in their various
rooms—including some at the top—but they have had small hope
beyond survival. If a girl is with the protagonist, she is usually either
the wrong one or a friend in desperation. *The Magus* leaves Nick

and Alison with an uncertain economic and social future. But the important hope which this novel leaves is that they have *chosen each other*—reasserting positive action in an age whose dilemma had almost ruled out any significant choice for its literary heroes except rejection.

CHAPTER 3

The Collector

I *Villain as Hero*

IN modern fiction, one does not find characters of undistilled evil.
Iris Murdoch's Gerald Scottow is about as diabolical as any, but
he is awfully polite about imprisoning the heroine, and it *is* his job,
and, it *is* for everyone's good, what with today's complexities.
Anthony Burgess's droogs get rough with the bicycle chains, but
malchicks have to tolchock something to release their razdraz at
being depersonalized by society—and they do like Beethoven.
Donleavy's Ginger Man gingerly breaks up bars and dental work,
and lower-class heroes like Arthur Seaton and Charles Lumley
smuggle dope, get in fistfights, and live lives of noisy desperation in
the name of man's reaction to absurd existence. If Godot is not
coming, they have decided to break up the waiting room.

Perhaps the last villains were William Golding's choirboys in *The
Lord of the Flies.* Huxley's Spandrell tried to be evil; James's Peter
Quint will not qualify unless we include ghosts. Perhaps it was
Faulkner's Popeye. Maybe it was Conrad's Gentleman Brown, Lord
Jim's archenemy. But three quarters of a century have elapsed since
Gentleman Brown escaped down river, and few convincing successors have surfaced in his wake. The best, or worst, villains we get
nowadays are likely to be blindly successful establishment figures
who do the hero out of his individuality. And the hero is not evil; if
he acts irrationally, it is his only alternative to complete passivity in
a system that precludes the individual act.

We have found ourselves rooting for the sometimes irrational
antihero because of his picaresque charm, our sympathy for the
underdog, and the twentieth-century man's longing to reestablish a
situation in which he can act decisively. That longing for *action* to be
restored has not escaped even the most rational of modern men, and
we see it made manifest in the impulse of popular culture to reassert

73

unmitigated heroism and unmitigated villainy in subliterature and cinema. We glorify Batman and Robin and exult in their totally wicked foes; we heap nostalgia on the days of Tom Mix and Gene Autrey, when we could spot the bad guys by their hats, like jerseys in a football game. We delight in the victory of trim, young James Bond over sloppy, lecherous Goldfinger. Strangely enough, we do not really mind very much when Bond kicks below the belt and slaps the girls around a bit. He is still the hero, and we are on his side. We begin to admire the well-intentioned hero who is willing to use nasty tactics on the side of virtue. We name him "Dirty Harry," and we are reassured to see him blaze away *in our behalf* with a forty-four magnum. Barely a cut above jamesbondishness is the epic-*length* novel of the Harold Robbins school, whose hero, steeped in self-righteous anger, justifies any means of attacking forces which oppose him. And we like it.

Such grasping for action at the price of morality even spills over into national attitudes. During World War II, Germany found it reassuring to absolutize issues and unite behind common racial hatreds. The United States has for some time found it convenient to identify God with free enterprise, Satan with communism, and Beelzebub with socialism. We of today take comfort in thus over-simplifying issues of good and evil. Finally we justify electing national leaders who have the one-dimensional courage to fight dirty in "our" behalf. With such a tendency underway, it took the intense moral outrage of a relatively few people to convince the United States that Nixonian amorality was, after all, immorality.

But the outlaw hero lurks deep in us all, as John Fowles shows in his essay "On Being English but Not British," and Fowles traces the impulse back to the Robin Hood legend: "He is the man who always, when faced with taking to the forest or accepting injustice, runs for the trees. Robinhoodism is essentially *critical opposition that is not content not to act.*"[1] Fowles says that robinhoodism ends when it emerges from the forest and takes power. I consider that development a variant of what freedom-minded Americans permitted between the 1960s and 1970s. Although the underdog bias in both Albion Englishness and our Columbian variety arises outside the establishment, its merger with our wish for decisive action made a paradox in popular political and literary tastes. Starved for momentum, we crypto-outlaws became too willing to justify dirty tricks in behalf of Good (which we had come to identify with national prosperity) against Evil (which we identified with any counterforce).

In literature, it was a short step from the humorous antihero to the *violent* antihero, and nobody seemed to mind very much. But now the "angry" fiction of the 1950s and part of the 1960s has been left behind in a return to a moral vision, although such novelists as Murdoch, Bellow, and Greene had never lost theirs. I do not mean to deprive the modern irrational antihero of the sympathy he deserves as fictional opponent of all our century's frustrations. But he had his licks in a symbolic barroom brawl that went on for over a decade, and it is nice to see that they are serving drinks again.

Fowles's *The Collector* may turn out to be the literary document that gave the violent antihero his *coup de grace*. In 1963, the novel appeared when sympathy for aberrant behavior was still strong in literature—the same year of Burgess's *A Clockwork Orange*, which shows the danger of eradicating man's aesthetic sense along with his violence. Perhaps Burgess's book, too, helped to destroy the violent antihero, stepping into the not-too-distant future for what may have been the ultimate statement possible by a novel generally sympathetic toward antiheroic violence. It was easy to befriend Keith Waterhouse's Billy Liar, who mentally mowed down antagonists with his imaginary Ambrosian repeater-gun. And we did not mind excusing Donleavy's Ginger Man for wrecking an occasional pub. But Alex's pleasure outings of rape and murder were hard to take. Lucky Jim had come full circle, and there was nowhere else to go.

Fowles's book is hardly as gory, but it is more subtly and profoundly chilling. And his antihero is more like Bluebeard than Robin Hood. Burgess's Alex is as much victim as criminal, another modern man trapped by class. But Fowles shows how class freedom conferred gratuitously upon Clegg suddenly makes him the *trapper*, not the trapped. True, Clegg is a soft-spoken monster spawned by generations of social inequality. Fowles makes his villain's disadvantage clear, but he does not diminish the loathesomeness of Clegg's crime. Fowles presents his character straightforwardly, showing a usually gentle young man with some consideration for his imprisoned beloved. The causes of his evil are clear; his thin virtues are clear; we sympathize with Clegg; but his crime is *no less evil*. We sympathize far more deeply with Miranda, whose horrible fate makes Clegg literature's first convincing villain since Conrad's Gentleman Brown. Society is not guiltless for Clegg's evil, and we recognize our link to Gentleman Brown just as his enemy Jim did.

But evil is unmitigated in Clegg, as it is unexcused in society for having formed his being. It is his *guilt* which is mitigated.

Despite the roundness of both the book's characters, they appeared amid times of great sympathy for the underdog, lower-class antihero. As a result, a few people, especially in England and close to the class conflict, interpreted the novel as a one-dimensional allegory slighting the lower class. But the vast majority of the reviews were very favorable, in both Britain and the United States—roughly eighty percent favorable, with a surprising concentration of praise from Britain's literary establishment. However, a significant number of both favorable and unfavorable reviews tended to sympathize with Clegg and reproach Fowles for allegedly favoring Miranda. The irony of that view is that Fowles's understanding characterization of Clegg had generated their sympathy in the first place, even given the epoch's predisposition to favor the lower-class hero. Only a few, however, took this line of criticism very far, and their greatest fallacy was identifying Fowles's viewpoint with Miranda's—assuming that he believes the liberal-modish clichés which he writes in her journal, as well as her occasional diatribes of class prejudice. But Fowles is too wise to let either of the characters become only a mouthpiece. Although Miranda's journal reveals a far more clear-sighted and virtuous character than Clegg's story shows, such a difference is biologically and socially inevitable. Not one review commented adversely on the characterization of Clegg, and many of them praised the novel's depth as well as its thriller value. Many recognized the book for the subtle masterpiece that it is, among them the reviewer for the *Times Literary Supplement:* "As a novel that is trying to make a serious moral statement and making it seriously and well, *The Collector* deserves attention, and the more so because Mr. Fowles brings to it the proper gifts of the novelist. His story-telling transcends the difficult and limited structure he has imposed on himself. His characterization is good, especially through Miranda's diary. This is already a haunting and memorable book, and it will be interesting to see how it wears."[2] Honor Tracy, herself a novelist, concluded in *The New Republic,* "It is early days to sound the trumpets, but it does look as if the new England has brought forth a novelist at last."[3] As things have turned out, she was right. And no small part of Fowles's reputation is due to his flawless characterization of Frederick Clegg.

II   *The Plot*

Clegg himself narrates the book's first part, explaining matter-of-factly how he, secretly and at a distance, becomes romantically obsessed with Miranda Grey, a pretty young daughter in a middle-class house across from Town Hall Annexe, where he is a rates clerk. He watches her from an office window and logs her appearances in his "entomological observations diary" along with sightings of butterflies. Throughout his unhappy and banal lower-class boyhood, his butterfly collecting has been his only contact outside the foster home where he supports his ignorant aunt and her spastic daughter. His only outlet is meeting with the "Bug Section" of a naturalist group, until he sights Miranda and daydreams an elaborate relationship with her. His fantasies begin to dominate his life when he wins a fortune in a football pool, leaves his job, and is left at his leisure. When his aunt and cousin take their cut of the money and go to Australia, Clegg, alone in a London hotel, turns increasingly to pornography. He takes up photographing butterflies, but also gets telephoto shots of lovers coupling in the country. At last he buys a remote seventeenth-century country house outside of Lewes and converts its secret Catholic chapel to an underground prison cell. Then, in his new van, outfitted especially for the hunt, he kidnaps Miranda as she walks home from her London art school. Chloroforming her as he does butterflies, he imprisons her in the subterranean room, furnished and stocked with clothes and art books especially for her. He has taken every precaution. She has no chance of escape or rescue.

Clegg tells of a strange relationship that develops between them—how he promises to release her in a month, then breaks his promise, how they argue over politics and art, how she attempts escape several times, then tries to disable him with an ax. At last she desperately offers him sex, but in angry humiliation at his impotence and self-righteous shock at her "fallen" state, he demands that she pose for seminude, then nude, photographs. He apparently masturbates with her photos just as he has with the nudie magazines, and the more she becomes his fantasy sex object, the less she remains his idealized princess. Although she becomes seriously ill, Clegg insists that she is feigning, as she had earlier while trying to escape. He binds, gags, and strips her and forces her to pose for his pictures; then he tries to cure her pneumonia with patent medicine. His narration breaks off without revealing Miranda's fate.

The second part of the novel is Miranda's viewpoint, recorded in the diary she had kept beneath her mattress. Revealing her to be sensitive and intelligent though occasionally immature, the diary also shows how frightened and determined she is. She had planned and hoped for days before each of the futile escape attempts that Clegg had mentioned in brief annoyance. The diary also reveals her personality and life—including a weak father, hostile mother, devoted sister, and pretentious aunt. The aunt, with whom she had lived in London, had introduced the twenty-year-old Miranda to George Paston, a forty-one-year-old painter. Miranda had admired G. P., as she calls him, for his art and eccentricity. Her diary shows how his attitudes have affected her own, and how she is attracted by the thought of an affair with him.

While Miranda hopes and schemes for freedom, she writes of the slow-witted Clegg, relating him to her feelings about social reform and brotherhood. She shows misgivings about using violence, then, after her abortive ax attack on Clegg, is repulsed by her own act. She tries to give him sex, then is puzzled by Clegg's fury at his impotence. Before falling ill, she appears changed by her ordeal, still caring for Clegg while railing against his insensitivity and that of other so-called New People. Miranda is determined to use her life creatively, even to risking a closer relationship with G. P. As her pneumonia interrupts the diary, she has abandoned faith in an intervening God, but she remains determined to live.

The third part of the book returns to Clegg's account of Miranda's illness and his failure to help her. Having rationalized that she is past help, he allows her to die in an upper bedroom, carefully locked though she was too weak to rise. Clegg arranges the corpse back down in her prison room, fails in his effort to make it smile, takes a lock of hair, says part of a prayer, and goes upstairs. Unable to sleep, he returns to the corpse and decides upon a romantic suicide, then goes back upstairs and sleeps soundly.

But in the brief fourth part of the book, Clegg recalls having awakened the next morning and abandoned his suicide plans—a decision he justifies, along with his entire crime, by his discovering her diary and its revelation that she had not loved him. Virtually without remorse, Clegg tells of burying her, then preparing her empty cell for another prisoner—a girl he is *only thinking about* as

Miranda's possible successor. But he is carefully and unconsciously beginning to fulfill his fantasy—again.

III *Clegg*

Dating from Greek tragedy, the best authors present their villains in sufficient depth to show what makes them evil; and in most cases, revealing villains' human qualities increases their power and appeal. Few novelists have drawn their agents of evil with the understanding Fowles shows for Clegg. Fowles gives the reader extensive knowledge of Clegg's childhood, particularly of Aunt Annie and Cousin Mabel, all he has left of a family. The two women have jealously combined forces against him. Aunt Annie is entirely too conscious of having taken him in as an orphan, and she tortures him with Mabel's handicap. While her letter warns him against depleting his fortune, the old woman still manages to mention his childhood indebtedness to her. Clegg, in return, betrays an almost emotionless attitude toward her and Mabel. Though apparently recognizing their greed, he quietly gives them a third of his fortune. He is relieved to be rid of them, and, although insensitive enough to advocate euthanasia for the likes of Mabel, he still prepares a room for their return. The great tragedy of his childhood had been the death of his Uncle Dick, the one person besides Miranda whom he remembered as he grasped the pool check. He at last has the means of giving to someone he cares about. Although he tries to buy Miranda's affection, he does offer to donate to her nuclear disarmament fund. His own account does not take credit for the idea, but Miranda's version shows that her own rebuff may have stifled his generosity. He might have sent the money had she not impugned his motives.[4] Several scenes generate more sympathy for Clegg than for Miranda. The strongest example of her insensitivity to his feeling happens when she embarasses him by saying his aunt has made him a fool. He fears that Miranda will abandon him to hating his own family, but she does not listen: "*Do* shut up. You're ugly enough without starting to whine. . . . [H]e was standing there with his mouth open, trying to say something. And I knew I'd hurt him" (199). Compounding the injury, Miranda patronizes Clegg with her "fairy story" of a princess imprisoned by a "very ugly monster," while her own captor gazes bitterly at the floor. The scene shows Clegg as human, as knowing that Miranda fails to understand his dilemma. When she offers him his turn at a fairy tale, he simply replies that he loves her—more an imaginative fantasy than either of them realizes.

His obsession with Miranda's image is pitiful, like his entire life: grieving for the lost uncle, feeling angrily inferior around others, and pathetically pursuing butterflies and pictures of nude women. He must rely upon his miserable "Bug Section" for meeting a "better class of people," and he cannot live happily even with a fortune in his hands. The money only gives him leisure to inflate his fantasies and power to fulfill them, however devastating they become. Analyzing the feelings she finally realizes he has, Miranda reaches the heart of his sickness when she compares his fixation to Dante's love for Beatrice. But she does not see how astute her own analogue is, though she does see that Dante's mania was creative while Clegg's is destructive. Dante's distant poetic devotion was like Alain-Fournier's creating a novel to his remote beloved, like the Great Gatsby's building an empire for his, like John Clare's poetic marriage to faraway Mary. Clegg is cursed with the same romantic obsession but not blessed with the creativity to feed it. His sad monument to Miranda is imprisoning her in his own perverted paradise. Had the lottery not thrust power upon Clegg's barren spirit, she would have remained his *princesse lointaine*, noted along with sightings of butterflies.

Clegg is pursuing the anima figure, the archetypal dream girl, as certainly as Nick pursues Lily in *The Magus* and Charles pursues Sarah in *The French Lieutenant's Woman*. The difference lies not only in social class; the tragic distinction is the intensity of Clegg's obsession, aggravated by his childhood's acute insecurity. Circumstance has forced insensitivity upon him, but it is his *sensitivity* which drives him into obsession with his fantasies, all of which revolve around poor Miranda. Too shy to feel comfortable even among his class, Clegg is a miserable and solitary figure. He makes Miranda's prison inescapable because he is too lonely to *trust* anyone. As he tells her, "You don't know what being alone is. . . . You're everything. I got nothing if you go" (271). As his loneliness deepens his fantasies, his insecurities bring him to monomaniacal possessiveness. He seeks to preserve fleeting beauty of butterflies by fixing them in death. Stunned by Miranda's beauty, he tries to possess her as well, likening her to an emerging imago he had "had to" kill. Clegg's morality is blurred by longing for beauty that eludes him. By imprisoning Miranda, he surrenders to his unconscious, his fantasy—the anima imago. Not only does "imago" identify both emerging insects and emerging art, but the term refers to an idealized mental image as well. Finally, Clegg also kills his anima imago, tragically projected upon Miranda.

IV *Clegg and Miranda*

Miranda is, to her sorrow, one of those women Jung considers a natural personification of the anima figure. This coincidental quality of hers prevents certain anima-obsessed men from regarding her as a real, conscious phenomenon. Even to a man as aware as G. P., she is likely to remain the dream girl, the faraway princess—a potentially destructive illusion. G. P. is aware of his own attraction to the anima as he subdues his feelings for Miranda. When she replies to G. P. that she has not read Jung, he tells her, "He's given your species of the sex a name. Not that it helps. The disease is just as bad" (187). Miranda does not make the connection, even when she concludes of Clegg, "I could never cure him. Because I'm his disease" (265). Jung describes her "disease" precisely.[5] The ideal quality in Miranda is the key to why Clegg is not attracted by her reality but instead, as she says, by "the way I look and speak and move" (89). As Clegg puts it, "Having her was enough. Nothing needed doing. I just wanted to have her, and safe at last" (101). Considering releasing her, he thinks not of her personality but of her *image:* "But then I thought of her face and the way her pigtail hung down a bit sideways and twisted and how she stood and walked and her lovely clear eyes. I knew I couldn't do it" (36). Unfortunately, only Miranda's looks and outward manner make her what she is to Clegg: a delusion which G. P. had fled. Reminding himself that she is not *the* ideal woman, but Jung's ideal-woman *type*, G. P. tells her that she would be a bore if she were not so pretty, then inscribes his drawing *"pour 'une' princesse lointaine,"* with the *"une"* heavily underlined (188).

Projecting the anima image upon Miranda, Clegg first idealizes her, reverently waits on her, and keeps her princess of his illusory kingdom. Although he photographs her, he is no simple voyeur. Clegg's great anxiety is her *living reality.* As long as she is alive to think, demand, contradict, hope, and feel, he cannot possess her "safe at last." Unconsciously to Clegg, achieving *complete safety* for his obsession would mean effacing all hazard and mystery by destroying life—as he has done with butterflies. He values life little:

his own is worthless enough. He justifies killing the new imago to possess its beauty; he even excuses tortures the Nazis "had to do." He thinks that spastics like his cousin should be "put out painlessly." He finally dreams of "having to" smother Miranda with a pillow rather than lose her.

But as long as Miranda remains idealized in Clegg's mind, he cannot rationalize mistreating her. His worshipful attitude is closely linked to sexuality. The thought of Miranda had rendered him impotent with a prostitute. In spite of his feeling guilty before her pure and idealized image, Clegg's pornography reassures him privately that he is not impotent. The more intimate his views and photographs of Miranda become, the more she loses the mystery essential to the anima figure. And the closer she becomes identified with his sexuality, the less pure and perfect she is. Her image takes its first damaging blow on the night he chloroforms her and photographs her in her underwear. Clegg has come a long way from having "every respect," and as he says, "Things were never the same again" (92). Even so, he still maintains self-righteously that he is "not that sort at all," because in his puritanical mind, violating Miranda is still like incestuously raping the mother-virgin-anima-goddess figure.

But in Clegg's romantic fantasy it is a short step from hero to villain, avenging knight to jealous dragon, rescuer to attacker— although he is not conscious of reversing his roles. He speaks of the day he first "gave" himself the dream of abducting her. He begins the dream as her rescuer, becomes attacker, then gentle captor: "Here I kept her in a nice way." At that stage, Clegg's fantasy had been as innocent as Peter Pumpkin Eater's "there he kept her very well"—the archetypal impulse to confine the object of desire harmlessly. But at the opposite pole of that same old motif is Poe's Roderick Usher—who had not realized what he was doing either.

To be violent, Clegg must devise some reason to rationalize his act. Sadly enough for Miranda, her attempt to give him sexual tenderness furnishes the self-justifying mechanism he has unconsciously sought. Even her ax attack had not provoked him to violence; only her sexual degradation sullies her image enough to warrant, in his mind, real cruelty. He is furious at her seeing his impotence, and now he can excuse punishing her for tainting his ideal. He says that he could have killed Miranda even then, that his later acts were because of the incident, and that he never respected her again. Defending his virility, he takes greater refuge in his photographs: "I could take my time with them. They didn't talk back at me" (109). Not only has Clegg granted himself license to assimilate Miranda into his grosser and unidealized fantasies, but he justifies partial surrender to his sex-linked sadism. Now he can gain sexual stimulation while avenging upon Miranda all his vast frustrations. Her "immorality" has betrayed her image, toppled her from the pedestal, and entitled him to *demand* further "art" poses of her. His irresolution has gone, and he feels righteous superiority, perverse vindictiveness: "even if it wasn't what she deserved in the beginning she had made it so that she did now. I had real reasons to teach her what was what" (114). When he binds and strips her for his photographs, he justifies himself as punisher: "I said, all right, I'm going to teach you a lesson" (117). In essence he has already managed to kill the living part of Miranda. He has the photographs—completely unidealized by now and merged with his sexual fantasies: "The best ones were with her face cut off" (118). He rationalizes that "it was her fault" for having feigned illness earlier and that he does not bring help because he "seemed to find reasons not to go" (292). He easily justifies his being frightened out of both attempts to reach a doctor. Clegg at last rationalizes even Miranda's death—congratulating himself on how hard he had taken it: "I was truly and really in despair, although I say it myself" (294). Nevertheless, he is tidying up downstairs to occupy his waiting for her to die above; then he treats himself to a cup of tea after closing her mouth and eyelids. The next morning, he abandons his brief notion of committing a romantic suicide, plans during breakfast how to dispose of the corpse, and by mid-morning has effaced virtually all remorse. He uses her diary's evidence that "she never loved me" to reinforce his guiltlessness. His self-righteous tone and the certainty that there is to be another "guest" give the same chilly feeling of "Porphyria's Lover" and "My Last Duchess." He has her lock of hair and the photographs; the *next* one will be more manageable— one he can "teach."

Several times both Clegg and Miranda use the terms "mad" and "madness" to describe his condition. The quality and degree of Clegg's insanity depend primarily upon whether the analysis is behavioral, Jungian, Freudian, or some other. No matter what terminology one applies to Clegg, his aberrant behavior is no less evil, and classifying it is no comfort. Fowles shows Clegg's mental illness to be symptomatic of a greater disease in society.

V *Miranda*

At society's opposite intellectual pole, Miranda shows different symptoms of its disease. On several occasions she fails to understand Clegg; she sometimes ignores his good impulses and embarrasses him for his ignorance. But the central fact which mitigates Miranda's hostility is his withholding her most valuable possession—freedom. He is keeping her from daylight, air, natural beauty she loves, people she loves. Her last painting was to have been a butter-yellow sunrise, and she dies reaching for the winter sun. The novel is not sentimental, but it does not show much to *blame* in Miranda. Her diatribes are rather to be expected from someone who has lost her freedom and gradually realizes that she may lose her life as well. As captive, her *talk* is sometimes hateful, but she is best judged by *actions*. Clegg does not *talk* hate very much; he *acts* it. No matter how futile one may think Miranda's protest marching and fund-raising, they are at least *moral actions based upon moral feelings*. Faced with the H-bomb question, Clegg only cites the individual's impotence to change social injustice—a powerlessness he understands far better than Miranda does. But she understands what Clegg can hardly be expected to comprehend: the importance of feeling and acting upon one's feelings. She tries unsuccessfully to explain by introducing the militaristic-but-honest American sergeant into her argument, which Clegg squelches with, "I thought we were talking about the H-bomb" (143). Both of them are making valid points—Clegg about individual powerlessness and Miranda about acting upon feelings in spite of powerlessness. Miranda understands the issue's complexity, but she congratulates herself a bit too warmly for her symbolic action: "we do it to keep our self-respect to show to ourselves, each one to himself or herself, that we care. And to let other people, all the lazy, sulky, hopeless ones like you, know that someone cares" (142). Miranda continues shaming Clegg even when he offers money for her cause, the only positive *action* he can conceive. She can launch extended harangues typical of intellec-tualism's worst prejudices: "I hate the uneducated and the ignor-ant. . . . I hate all ordinary dull little people who aren't ashamed of being dull and little." Miranda sometimes fancies herself among the Few, "a sort of band of people who have to stand against all the rest. . . . famous men, dead and living, who've fought for the right things and created and painted in the right way, and unfamous people I know who don't lie about things, who try not to be lazy, who try to be human and intelligent." Miranda's introspection is fair: "I'm vain. I'm not one of them. I *want* to be one of them, and that's not the same thing" (221–24). But Miranda's talk of her own freedom from class prejudice sometimes sounds like protesting too much. She brags of lower-class friends while railing against the New People, whom she usually criticizes astutely despite now and then generalizing shortsightedly.

G. P.'s snobbery is more vicious than Miranda's. Even when he criticizes anti-intellectualism accurately, he is far too brutal, and Miranda sometimes admires him for the wrong reasons. She is impressed by his having insulted a miner's son so forcefully that the working-class youth had admitted defeat. But Miranda's admiring G. P. is not entirely unjustified. He is rightly indignant at pretentiousness, and some of his views are wise; part of his influence upon Miranda has been productive. His most honest act had been to admit his own immaturity and reject her so that he would not involve her further in his life. Such apparent unselfishness had probably not been part of some ultimate seduction scheme, since he is honest about his own flaws and her role as *a* princess instead of *the* one. At other times, he enjoys playing aesthetic pundit too much, with such poses as his sacred music-listening position, prone on the couch. And one can hardly excuse his cruelty to the working-class boy who had mistakenly valued G. P.'s contempt.

An important virtue of *The Collector* is that Fowles does not cheat. Clegg speaks in his lower-class clichés, and Miranda and G. P. speak in their middle-class ones; Fowles presents both bad and good qualities of each class, resisting any urge to "prettify" characters, as Miranda accuses Alan Sillitoe of doing to his lower-class hero. Fowles calls his own novel an analysis of evil produced by class conflict: "Clegg, the kidnapper, committed the evil; but I tried to show that his evil was largely, perhaps wholly, the result of a bad education, a mean environment, being orphaned: all factors over which he had no control. In short, I tried to establish the virtual *innocence* of the Many."[6] Fowles does not fully accept my earlier assertion that Clegg's *guilt*, rather than his *evil*, is mitigated; Fowles's biological view is too aware of determining forces not to question my moralism: "I think you put the situation over Clegg (my view of him) neatly and well, though of course it begs a question: whether unmitigated evil that can't help itself is as evil as that which can. I suppose Claggart in *Billy Budd* . . . is the type example of this wilful kind of evil. Iago, possibly. [The issue] in turn begs all kinds of questions, philosophically—for [they are] at least shown to choose evil freely by the author. But certainly I think the Clegg-like kind of person in British society is largely conditioned."[7] Fowles explains in *The Aristos* that Miranda has little more control over what she is than Clegg has over his own destiny—but that she might have grown out of her priggishness and arrogance to become "the kind of being humanity so desperately needs. The actual evil in Clegg overcame the potential good in Miranda" (A, 10).

The Collector comes to a shocking and desolate end. It is a modern tragedy (not a loose use of the word), but Fowles insists that its bleakness does not mean that he regards the future with pessimism,

> nor that a precious *elite* is threatened by the barbarian hordes. I mean simply that unless we face up to this unnecessarily brutal conflict (based largely on an unnecessary envy on the one hand and an unnecessary contempt on the other) between the biological Few and the biological Many; unless we admit that we are not, and never will be, born equal, though we are all born with equal human rights; unless the Many can be educated out of their false assumption of inferiority and the Few out of their equally false assumption that biological superiority is a state of existence instead of what it really is, *a state of responsibility*—then we shall never arrive at a more just and happier world. (A, 10)

Fowles believes in partial biological determinism as well as in the exercise of some free will. "Hazard, the great factor we shall never be able to control, will always infest life with inequality. And it seems madness that man himself should continue blindly to propagate this vicious virus in our world instead of trying to limit it" (A, 11).

There are several principal ironies to this story of Miranda and her strange Ferdinand. The first is the intensity of Clegg's fantasy; his deed begins not as evil, but as what he calls "the best thing I ever did." The second irony is the football pool, which Fowles classifies in *The Aristos:* "Lotteries, football pools, bingo games and the rest are the chief protection of the modern rich against the furies of the modern poor. One hangs from the lamp-post the person one hates; not the person one wants to be" (A, 126). But the pool's gratuitous fortune is not enough for Clegg, who says that he wanted "what money couldn't buy." He had already tried to buy happiness in a Soho brothel. For Miranda, the most tragic irony is her kindness which changes Clegg into a monster instead of the prince she seeks: "Perhaps I should be his dream-girl. . . . More than kiss him. Love him. Make Prince Charming step out" (254). But Clegg is *not* Ferdinand, in spite of his fancies; neither is he exactly like Caliban, in spite of Miranda's clever conceit: "Whom stripes may move, not kindness," who, unhampered in his rape attempt, "had peopled else / This isle with Calibans" (263). Instead, Clegg's own inferior feelings paralyze him into impotence. The football pools are, as Miranda writes, very like the power with which Stephano and Trinculo tempt Caliban, but there the similarity to *The Tempest* ceases. Shakespeare's Caliban, his foolish ambition thwarted, says, "I'll be wise hereafter" (263). But there is no intervening power to prevent Clegg from carrying out his evil. That is the final irony. There is no Prospero in this story.

VI *The Isolated World*

Miranda's hopeless situation intensifies the sense of man's isolation from his fellows and from any intervening force, a feeling characteristic of Fowles's fiction. Miranda's airtight ten-by-ten-by-twenty-foot cell is the most claustral of all his settings, intensifying the interdependence of the two characters' one-sided symbiosis: Clegg draws upon Miranda psychologically while she depends upon him for her very physical existence. Both remain totally isolated from others: Clegg even on his trips to town and Miranda even when Clegg allows her out of her room, bound and gagged. Fowles's setting in *The Collector* is the sort of ultimate isolation which has appealed to imaginations of writers for many decades, as Fowles himself says:

It is the dramatic psychosexual implications of isolating extreme situations that excite and interest me. . . . In *The Collector* I tried to write in terms of the strictest realism; to go straight back to that supreme master of the fake biography, Defoe, for the surface "feel" of the book. To Jane Austen and Peacock, for the girl. To Sartre and Camus, for the "climate." . . . Imprisonment as only the most extreme of a whole group of allied situations: the stuck lift (as used brilliantly by Bergman in *A Lesson in Love*), the shipwreck or aircrash (Golding), the desert island (Defoe to Antonioni), the jungle, the yacht, the room (Ionesco and Pinter), the lonely house (the Brontës), the car in the fog, and so on.[8]

Clegg's and Miranda's exile from both mankind and divine intervention also underlines the need for each person to become a

creator—a novelist, a god, as it were, who somehow *realizes* the
world that *is* by making a fictional one as real as the existing one. In
the way Fowles describes in his famous thirteenth chapter of *The
French Lieutenant's Woman,* his protagonists create *fictions* which
reconcile their personal lot with external reality. Conchis frees
Nicholas with dramatic fiction; Sarah frees herself—and finally
Charles—by assuming the fictional role of outcast; Isobel Dodgson's
enigma lies in the novel she is writing; the inarticulate thief of "Poor
Koko" wants his own story written; Daniel Martin writes his novel;
but Clegg *lives* a tragic fiction, a fancied romantic hero who is really
a grotesque villain. Miranda's diary shows her working out her own
reality through a sort of fiction; her memory cannot be perfect, and
she occasionally admits narrative cheating in her own behalf. Even
her rendering of Clegg's speech sounds less awkward than his own
narration. Fowles presents Miranda's journal subtly, revealing her
character and background, and showing how, during her writing,
her hesitance develops into readiness to face hazard: "I've always
tried to happen to life; but it's time I let life happen to me" (258).
Her decision to attempt sex with Clegg, however disastrous, is
evidence of her maturing attitude. She has stopped being appalled
by G. P.'s sexuality and is willing to risk an affair with him just to
test the love that she suspects may be there, because she now knows
that love matters more than sex. In working out her fiction, she
admits her own pretenses, corrects her own pomposity, and, despite her growing fear, is able to appreciate existence and love. Her
lack of freedom and her failure with Clegg have shown her beauty in
all love, even purely sexual: "The only thing that is ugly is this
frozen lifeless utter lack-love between Caliban and me" (265). She
finally is able to discard completely her old "Ladymont" self, her
middle-class pettiness, and her artistic arrogance as well. She
realizes that it is she, not her working-class friends, who needs
"lameducking": "I pick up my old self and I see it's silly. A toy I've
played with too often" (266). Working out her life in writing even
during its final ordeal has prepared her to risk deeper relationships
and greater achievements. Her fiction has used a variety of forms:
letters to those she loves, comments on herself and her world,
remembered dialogues, and simple lists of her thoughts. At last she
decides to *be,* despite the consequences: "I shall be hurt, lost,
battered and buffeted. But it will be like being in a gale of light,
after this black hole" (266). Fowles, in *The Aristos,* mentions three

main reasons for the artist's creating: "His simplest purpose is to describe the outer world; his next is to express his feelings about that outer world, and his last is to express his feelings about himself" (A, 189). Miranda's journal helps her to an amplified self-recognition by serving all three purposes. The tragedy is that she cannot live what her ordeal has taught her.

Even Clegg's fictional narration, adorned with prejudice and rationalization and limited by ignorance and forgetfulness, is his working out feelings by recounting his life. Miranda uses her narration to *expose* her old self; Clegg uses his as a self-justification so complete that it blinds him to his own evil. His narration seems to be an interior monologue, with few uses of the second person, none in direct address. He intends no obvious audience, even announcing his next scheme, and he is hardly contrite enough to be confessing. His narration appears to be Clegg's inner thoughts, complete with schoolbook morality and working-class clichés. Like Miranda's diary, Clegg's words seem a personal process not intended for a third party. Both accounts firmly distinguish their respective narrators, revealing first whether captor and captive are being honest with themselves.

Although there is no intervening deity, both Clegg and Miranda are ambivalent about their own isolation from God. In spite of his avowed atheism, Clegg recites a partial prayer over Miranda's corpse because "it seemed right," and although Miranda had already renounced her earlier faith in prayer, her delirious writings end by hopelessly pleading to God for her life. Her death is Fowles's final reminder that natural laws are not suspended upon request. In Fowles, the only numinous act is the individual's making enough sense of his own existence to use it lovingly—a resolution process very like an author's devising a fictional world. By so reconciling themselves to their own realities, Fowles' characters are able to exercise valid existentialist choice. Miranda's offering sexual love to Clegg may be viewed as that sort of decision. And her further resolution to risk happiness and security for creativity and love is evidence that Miranda might have continued in a more complete existence. Instead she dies with her new awareness—a victim of Clegg, who, incapable of *conscious* choice, drifts unawares toward a repetition of his crime: "I only put the stove down there today because the room needs drying out anyway" (305).

Although Fowles commented in his 1968 preface to *The Aristos* that Clegg's disadvantaged background had shown the Many to be innocent, his earlier statements about the novel reveal his profound concern with the predicament of the artist in modern society:

all the creative acts of preacher-artists (their declarations about themselves and their artefacts) are suspect—every false or clumsy move they make is pounced on as hypocrisy, as arrogance, as naivety—and the pressures on them, inner as well as outer, are all such as destroy whatever authenticity they have tried to establish in their ways of living and writing—and this is so, whether they are in economic terms "successes" or "failures." When Miranda talks about the Few, in *The Collector,* these are the kind of people I mean her to mean; preeminently creators, not simply highly intelligent or well-informed people; nor people who are simply skilled with words. . . . Heracleitos: the Few and the Many (the *aristoi* and the *polloi*); the attitude the Few must take. Heracleitos first saw the predicament that fascinates me: the intelligent trapped in the world of the stupid.[9]

In *The Collector,* this entrapment of the intelligent is not simply a matter of banal humanity smothering the artist. The main tension is the powerlessness of creative intellect in a society where the real issues are not even being contested. The biological disparity is between the intelligent and the ignorant, but the fighting is between the haves and the have-nots. As an artist, Miranda is really at neither pole in the materialistic war; that is why her tragedy is so intense. She seeks freedom to create, but falls victim to society's economic struggle.

CHAPTER 4

The French Lieutenant's Woman

I *The Novel's Genesis*

HALF-WAKING on an autumn morning in 1966, John Fowles first envisioned the woman who was to become his most famous heroine. The hypnopompic image which came to his bed at Underhill Farm outside Lyme Regis was that of a solitary woman gazing seaward from a deserted harbor wall. Fowles tried to ignore the recurring vision, but the nameless woman finally lured his interest away from other writing. The mysterious figure, Fowles recalls, seemed to have the vaguely romantic quality of another age:

The woman obstinately refused to stare out of the window of an airport lounge; it had to be this ancient quay—as I happen to live near one, so near that I can see it from the bottom of my garden, it soon became a specific ancient quay. The woman had no face, no particular degree of sexuality. But she was Victorian; and since I always saw her in the same static long shot, with her back turned, she represented a reproach on the Victorian Age. An outcast. I didn't know her crime, but I wished to protect her. That is, I began to fall in love with her. Or with her stance. I didn't know which.[1]

Though Fowles went on to give the vision a name, a face, and finally an entire history, he guarded her mystery. His hero Charles also wonders whether he is falling in love with Sarah or with her stance—her back turned upon hypocrisy. By protecting her, as Fowles had wanted to, Charles becomes an outcast himself. But he will never again be his old Victorian self.

In *The French Lieutenant's Woman*, Sarah Woodruff is exiled from proper Victorian society, but she typifies the growing breed of women gaining emancipation during the late nineteenth century, the time of this novel. Fowles is fascinated by the emergence of this faintly masculinized Victorian female, another of whom he describes in introducing a reprint of Sabine Baring-Gould's Victorian novel

Mehalah. Baring-Gould's heroine, far less genteel and mysterious than Sarah, is a lower-class woman of the 1870s, the decade immediately following the three-year time span of *The French Lieutenant's Woman:*

Mehalah herself stands for the "new woman" of the Late Victorian period. She has strong Pre-Raphaelite undertones, and strong sociological ones, for she is metaphorically trying to break from the tight stays (how symbolic that Guernsey sweater!) of masculine wishful thinking about woman's humble role in life. There is, as with so many of Rossetti's female faces, a distinctly masculine cast about her. . . . This was the new taste of the time—we see it in Swinburne, in countless others. The demure moppets of the 1850s and 60s were fast going out of fashion. . . . We can learn a great deal about the contemporary—and very confused—masculine attitude to women from this tempestuous Carmen of the Essex marshes. Swinburne, indeed, greatly admired Mehalah. . . .[2]

Fowles leaves his own heroine living with Swinburne and the Pre-Raphaelites in the summer of 1869. Sarah's liberation has placed her among the avant-garde, and she shares Mehalah's independent spirit. Sarah's mannish black jacket is as symbolic as the Essex woman's Guernsey sweater, but beyond opposing society's injustice, Sarah resembles Mehalah no closer than she does other ancestors, such as Hardy's distressed women.

Fowles considers Sarah closer kin to the black heroine of Claire de Durfourt's nineteenth-century French novel *Ourika.* Both Sarah and Ourika suffer male discrimination; education isolates both from native class; and the African heroine is doubly oppressed for her race, as Sarah is for embracing the role of scarlet woman. Fowles is so fond of *Ourika* that he has published his own English translation. His foreword to the limited edition sees Sarah's black clothing as a shade of the African woman's face—a parallel he realized months after finishing *The French Lieutenant's Woman:* "It came as a shock . . . to pick up *Ourika* one day and to recall that Charles was the name of the principal male figure there also. That set me to thinking. And though I could have sworn I had never had the African figure of Ourika herself in mind during the writing of *The French Lieutenant's Woman,* I am now certain in retrospect that she was very active in my unconscious."[3]

The French Lieutenant's Woman is about freeing modern humanity—not women alone, and existential awareness is even more central to this novel than to Fowles's previous two. Charles and Sarah emancipate themselves by understanding the existential dilemma eighty years before French philosophy defined it: "I am trying to show an existentialist awareness before it was chronologically possible. Kierkegaard was, of course, totally unknown to the British and American Victorians; but it has always seemed to me that the Victorian age, especially from 1850 on, was highly existentialist in many of its personal dilemmas. One can almost invert the reality and say that Camus and Sartre have been trying to lead us, in their fashion, to a Victorian seriousness of purpose and moral sensitivity." Fowles compares Victorian concern with Darwinism to modern worry over nuclear destruction. The more sensitive Victorians felt infinitely isolated, and, by the 1860s, some sensed the crumbling of social, religious, and philosophical structures. Charles and Sarah were among the few Victorians who looked into the void almost a century before Existentialism named it: "an existentialist before his time, walks down the quay and sees that mysterious back, feminine, silent, also existentialist, turned to the horizon."[4] Charles sees Sarah almost as she had appeared in her creator's dreamlike vision, but he suffers to discover the emptiness she was facing.

II *The Plot*

Fowles's narrator-persona shares that opening scene with the reader through the telescope of an unnamed "spy." Charles Smithson, a thirty-two-year-old London gentleman, is escorting his twenty-one-year-old fiancée, Ernestina Freeman, who had insisted upon defying the March wind on the Cobb. The narrator places the time as 1867 but dates himself in the twentieth century by comparing the old sea rampart to a contemporary Henry Moore sculpture.

Charles and Ernestina interrupt their upper-class repartee when they approach a black-clad woman staring seaward from the quay's extremity. Charles is fascinated as Tina tells of the outcast, known as "Tragedy" and "the French lieutenant's woman" (a euphemism for "whore"). Sarah Woodruff was reputedly seduced and abandoned by the shipwrecked French naval officer she had nursed to health in the home where she was governess. She has now been "taken in" by venomous Mrs. Poulteney, who displays the unfortunate girl to God and the Dorset gentry to prove her own Christian charity.

The next day, Charles, an amateur paleontologist, hunts fossils west of Lyme in the Edenic coastal landscape known as the Undercliff. Ernestina stays with her Aunt Tranter, a kind spinster with whom her parents have sent her to vacation away from London. To comfort Ernestina's boredom with Lyme's provinciality, Charles has taken rooms at a nearby inn. Leaving his servant Sam, who is smitten by Aunt Tranter's nubile maid, Mary, Charles picks his way along the rocky shoreline and then climbs into the maze of pathways in Ware Commons, the eastern half of the Undercliff. Seeking fossilized echinoderms on his way back to town, Charles finds Sarah sleeping on an isolated ledge below his path—not a fossil, but a new species instead. Awakened, she confronts Charles in surprise. With a formal apology, he leaves her alone.

But Charles is becoming obsessed with Sarah's silent mystery. As he stops for a bowl of milk at the Dairy, the dairyman damns the passing Sarah as "the French Loot'n'nt's Hoer." Charles overtakes her and offers to escort her to Lyme. She rejects his offer and asks that he not reveal her presence there, then goes on alone. Mrs. Poulteney has banned her from Ware Commons, a place of ill repute among the town's more pious. The following day, visiting at Mrs. Poulteney's, Charles and Aunt Tranter defend the rights of their servants Sam and Mary to associate with each other. He shares a glance of understanding with Sarah, who is present as a spectator. But when he encounters her again on the Undercliff, she is aloof as he offers to help free her from Mrs. Poulteney and Dorset. When Sarah protests that she has ties to the area, he assumes she refers to the French lieutenant. Replying that her seducer is married, Sarah leaves Charles wondering why she stays in Lyme.

Charles's thoughts begin to dwell upon Ernestina's shallowness, upon his own wanderlust, and, unconsciously, upon his sexual desire. As he continues his quest for fossils on Ware Commons, Sarah seeks him out. Meeting him in a tunnel of ivy, she gives him two of the fossils, known as "tests," and leaves, with the plea that he meet her there again to hear of her involvement with the French officer. Charles finishes the day over hot grog and cheroots with Dr. Grogan, Lyme's scholarly bachelor physician, who shares Charles's humanitarianism and his admiration for Darwin. But Charles's Darwinism takes the form of broad scientific curiosity and the assurance that he himself is one of the naturally selected.

Justifying his interest in Sarah as a humanitarian and scientific undertaking, Charles meets her again in the green tunnel, from where she leads him to a secluded bower and tells how Lieutenant

Varguennes had proposed marriage and lured her to Weymouth. Finding him in a disreputable inn, she had recognized the rake that he was, but she tells Charles she had submitted sexually to Varguennes despite her revulsion. She characterizes her act as marrying shame to isolate herself from her hopeless social trap. Too sensitive and well-educated to endure bondage of class and sex, she had chosen social ostracism to free herself from having to conform. The arrival of Sam and Mary forces Sarah and Charles to hide in the vines, from whose concealment they watch the lovers. To Charles's astonishment, Sarah turns from watching Sam kissing Mary and smiles unmistakably at him, stripping away social falsehood and suggesting her physical attraction to him. Flustered Charles retreats into formality, and he and Sarah leave separately.

That evening Charles is called to the country estate of his wealthy old Uncle Robert, who announces his own approaching marriage to a widow young enough to produce an heir and deprive Charles of inheriting the family estate and the baronetcy. Ernestina later takes the news with middle-class vulgarity, further undermining Charles's confidence in their engagement. That evening he tells Grogan of Sarah's asking that he meet her near the Dairy; she has gone alone to the Undercliff after being discharged by Mrs. Poulteney for having been seen passing the Dairy after her last meeting with Charles. Grogan guesses the truth—that she had intentionally shown herself, with the plan of being dismissed and throwing herself on Charles's mercy. The two men agree that Grogan should meet her in Charles's stead, and the doctor gives Charles a volume documenting case histories of female hysteria, supporting his intention to have Sarah treated for the mental disorder. But Charles reverses his decision and, contrary to the agreement, leaves at dawn ahead of Grogan to meet Sarah himself. He finds her in an isolated barn, where she admits that she has intentionally gotten herself dismissed. She entices Charles into an embrace, but he pushes away in mid-kiss and rushes from the barn—only to confront Sam and Mary, who also see Sarah before she can slip back from the doorway. The departing servants swear to keep the secret, but they burst into laughter when out of sight. Charles parts with Sarah, having given her money to live on. She takes rooms in the Endicott Family Hotel at Exeter, then sends Charles her address.

Charles, in London to reaffirm his marriage contract, feels fossilized by circumstances, after Ernestina's father has pressured him to join his large retail business. After a night of drinking at his club, then at a fancy brothel, Charles finds himself with a prostitute. Having just gotten into bed, he vomits when she tells him that her name is Sarah.

With his hangover the following morning, Charles receives Sarah's three-word message: Endicott Family Hotel. On the train to Exeter, where he is to take a coach back to Lyme Regis, Charles thinks of Sarah at the hotel, but resolves to forget her and return to Ernestina. The novel then ends in a thoroughly Victorian manner: the married pair blessed with children, Charles become a businessman, Aunt Tranter and Grogan prospering, Sam and Mary multiplying happily ever after, and, as a final justice, Mrs. Poulteney plunged to her proper hereafter.

But then the narrator reveals that the traditional ending is only how Charles *imagines* it. Things really have happened quite another way. Much earlier, in chapter 13, the narrator had broken into his own fiction to remind the reader that it is all merely a novel and that he is its author. Like a modern novelist, he had withheld his heroine's inner thoughts, though revealing those of other characters. Now the reader discovers that Charles had not taken the coach from Exeter that night; he had sent Sam to install him in the local inn, while he headed for the Endicott Family Hotel. Sam, hoping to blackmail Charles, reads Sarah's address, shadows Charles, and watches him enter Sarah's hotel.

Sarah is prepared for Charles's arrival, having feigned a sprained ankle so that the landlady would send him up to her room instead of calling her down. She is even wearing a newly bought shawl and nightgown for the occasion. Before he arrives, she has built a fresh mound in the coalgrate, and, during their halting reunion, coals fall out and ignite the blanket around her legs. When he has smothered the fire and is replacing the blanket, she touches his hand. From that point on, nature takes over and Charles carries her to bed. Afterward, he discovers blood which reveals that she had not given herself to Varguennes. Sarah admits her lie and sends him away. Alone and puzzled, Charles enters a church and has an epiphany in which he begins to see Sarah's reality instead of her ideal image just as he sees the humanity of Jesus instead of his martyrdom. Resolving to marry Sarah, he goes to his hotel and writes her of his new decision, but Sam opens the letter instead of delivering it. When Charles returns from Lyme to Exeter after the next day's agony of breaking his engagement and completely alienating himself, he finds Sarah gone. When Charles embarks upon a desperate search for her, he encounters the disguised narrator in their shared train compartment. While Charles dozes, the author surreptitiously considers his fate and decides to show two possible endings to the story.

Narrowly escaping legal revenge for his breach of promise, Charles despairs of finding Sarah and, leaving the search to private investigators, finds America his new spiritual home. At last his solicitor notifies him that Sarah has been found in London. The anonymous word of her whereabouts has come from Sam, now happily married to Mary, with two children and a job in the Freeman retail store. Sam feels guilty enough to help Charles quietly after Mary notices Sarah entering a Chelsea residence. Charles takes passage back and goes to the house, at 16 Cheyne Walk. A young woman admits him and, before taking him up to Sarah, consults a man who appears with a pen in his hand. Charles recognizes John Ruskin, the art critic, as he is led past an open door. Sarah appears dressed in bright avant-garde style. When she confirms Ruskin's identity and mentions Swinburne, Charles realizes the residence belongs to Pre-Raphaelite artist and poet Dante Gabriel Rossetti, whom he had seen downstairs. In Rossetti's studio, where an easel holds "The Blessed Damozel," Sarah explains that she is his secretary and model. Charles is shocked at the Pre-Raphaelites' scandalous popular reputation. Sarah reveals her alias, "Mrs. Roughwood," which she had assumed to escape being traced. She declares that she will never marry and resists his pleading. Finally, when Charles denounces her cruelty and turns to leave, she reveals their daughter, Lalage, born from their brief union. The three are reunited in a touching domestic scene.

Meanwhile, across Cheyne Walk, the amused narrator leans on the Thames parapet; having doffed his earlier disguise as stern evangelist, now he appears bedizened like an impresario, who sets his watch fifteen minutes backward, summons his landau, and rides away lounging in the seat. Inside the house, the dialogue between Charles and Sarah resumes where it had been fifteen minutes before, but now there is no Lalage to effect the happy ending. As Charles turns angrily to leave, Sarah stops him with her wordless smile, suggesting an unmarried friendship which might promise a physical relationship. But Charles leaves the house and walks away in anguish as the author's landau disappears in the distance.

III   *The Novel's Historical Quality*

At its elementary level, *The French Lieutenant's Woman* is a magnificent historical novel. It is the story of a Dorset farm girl whose strange revolt against Victorian convention frees her for a womanhood among the Pre-Raphaelites in London, while toppling an intelligent young gentleman from the upper class into exile. It is also the story of a city valet and a provincial housemaid who succeed in marriage and mercantilism, of a scholarly old bachelor physician, of a kind old spinster aunt, of a frivolous London girl whose wealth has barely failed to spoil her, and of a bigoted old widow who thinks Heaven operates on the points system. The novel's panorama of Victorian England bears close-ups of such specialized activities as London whoring and legal negotiating. The book documents discussions of Victorian science, politics, economics, and social custom, and it describes both urban and pastoral England. Such illumination is expected of a historical novel, and this one provides it. But *The French Lieutenant's Woman* is far more than a historical novel.[5] Fowles denies interest in that genre and does not consider this book part of it.[6] He compares it to other artists' using earlier form and technique: "Stravinsky's eighteenth-century rehandlings, Picasso's and Francis Bacon's use of Velasquez. But in this context words are not nearly so tractable as musical notes or brush-strokes."[7] Prokofieff's *Classical Symphony* ran through his mind as he wrote the novel, and he must feel his technique's kinship to Prokofieff's early twentieth-century renovation of mid-eighteenth-century classical style. Both Fowles and Prokofieff handled forms of previous centuries with loving irony. Fowles describes the central painting in "The Ebony Tower" as growing out of "a homage and a kind of thumbed nose to a very old tradition," a phrase he might also have applied to his own earlier book.[8] Such artistic use of outmoded form is not purely parody or pastiche, terms implying some disrespect for the model; nor is such reworking simply imitation or emulation, words suggesting parasitic cribbing. *The French Lieutenant's Woman*, like the *Classical Symphony,* is an original modern expansion upon older traditional forms. Written both admiringly and ironically, both works pay tribute to past techniques while gently spoofing them.

Because some of Fowles's effects blend epochs a century apart, there is temptation to call them anachronisms. His technique occasionally resembles Bernard Shaw's sicking ancient Egypt's Ra upon his British audience or Mark Twain's transporting his Connecticut Yankee back to Camelot. Fowles's narrator, in many ways a character as well, is part Fowles himself and part device. Since this author-persona is a modern novelist who slips into his own created past, his time-linking effects appear deceptively anachronistic. But his appearances in the novel are more synchronistic than anachronistic, since he remains obviously the twentieth-century novelist, merely disguised as Victorian for trips into the book—complete with contemporary transportation and timepiece. Such synchronic elements establish the perpetuity of existence and carry the theme of evolution: "Mary's great-great-granddaughter, who is twenty-two years old this month I write in, much resembles her ancestor; and her face is known over the entire world, for she is one of the more celebrated younger English film actresses."[9] The narrator carries out this sense of sempiternality by including such specifics as Ernestina's birth in 1846 and her death on the day the Nazis invaded Poland (1 September 1939). Such references link fictional characters to known reality in recent history, and the device is neither anachronistic nor hard to believe, since people often live ninety-three years. The author's toby jug which once belonged to Sarah, the Undercliff from the air, Mrs. Poulteney as inhabitant of the "Victorian Valley of the Dolls," today's public urinal replacing yesterday's Assembly Rooms—all such details destroy the separateness of the two ages and support Fowles's attitude toward existence as a horizontal concept without beginning or end. Such linking elements not only demonstrate his concept of time but also intensify the authenticity, the reality of his story.

IV   *The Intrusive Author*

Fowles fuses the old ingressive and omniscient point of view with his modernity as another way of showing the continuum of time. He also uses that traditional narrative technique to accomplish feats unavailable to contemporary novelists who refuse the old omniscience. In the process, he makes considerable fun of the tradition which has in recent decades come to insist that the author himself be ousted from his own fiction. Fowles ironically protests that the modern novelist (in the age of Robbe-Grillet and Barthes, leaders in the form-obsessed *nouveau roman* school) must give his characters freedom; then he rides smugly into his own fiction as novelist-god to parody the notion of an intervening deity. He is intervening in the name of nonintervention.

The question of the novelist's role is inseparable from the idea of God's, and this book's central concern with narrative point of view is as theological as it is literary. His ironic treatment notwithstanding, Fowles is quite serious about the godlike function performed by creators of fiction. Whatever narrative technique an author uses, it is ultimately impossible for him to avoid being omniscient and omnipotent in his own fiction; he knows his own creation and may share it as he likes. But because twentieth-century man no longer sees himself as manipulated by an intervening god, the modern novelist who hopes to create a believable world must avoid the appearance that he as creator can know and control that world. Since an omnipotent god no longer pulls the strings, today's novelist considers himself presumptuous if he seems to do so. Such was not the case in the Victorian novel, as Thackeray's conclusion to *Vanity Fair* illustrates: "Let us shut up the box and the puppets, for our play is played out."[10] Fowles directly contradicts Thackeray's metaphor:

Perhaps you suppose that a novelist has only to pull the right strings and his puppets will behave in a lifelike manner; and produce on request a thorough analysis of their motives and intentions. . . . The novelist is still a god, since he creates (and not even the most aleatory avant-garde modern novel has managed to extirpate its author completely); what has changed is that we are no longer the gods of the Victorian image, omniscient and decreeing; but in the new theological image, with freedom our first principle, not authority. (95–97)

Although Fowles mentions the leaders of the *nouveau roman,* his antipathy to their style-consciousness is well known. And his return to Victorian narrative is partly a mockery of their transmitting novels almost entirely through sensory perceptions of their characters. As if to emphasize that the modern novelist *does* exist in his fiction, Fowles returns unreservedly to the previous century's intrusiveness— editorializing, footnoting, quoting prose and poetry at will, taking every license of omnisience, even surpassing Trollope by writing himself into the plot, complete with physical description.

Nonetheless, in his jarring thirteenth chapter, Fowles also preserves his own theological image of god-novelist by rejecting omnipotence and refusing to trespass upon Sarah's inner mind: "There is only one good definition of God: the freedom that allows other freedoms to exist. And I must conform to that definition" (97). Fowles could have chosen *not* to conform to that image;[11] his refusing to do so betrays the seriousness behind his irony. In *The Aristos*, he presents the same theology: that "god" is a situation rather than a power, being, or influence—and that man's freedom proves the situation's sympathy despite its general indifference to the individual: "Freedom of will is the highest human good; and it is impossible to have both that freedom and an intervening divinity."[12]

One reason *The French Lieutenant's Woman* succeeds is Fowles's using the old omniscient and intrusive point of view with such grand style. Having established theoretical freedom of his characters, Fowles proceeds to assume the older technique with boldness which uses its best qualities. The result is so pleasant as to cast doubt upon some of today's avant-garde techniques. The current aversion to authorial involvement, especially as seen in the *nouveau roman*, has so limited narrative technique that such critics as Wayne C. Booth and Norman Friedman question its validity and defend advantages of omniscient narrative. Today's proponents of authorial detachment defend their principles in the name of artistic illusion, as if the reader is supposed to forget he is holding a book, which someone must have written. Fowles, using the intrusive method unavailable to them, anticipates their criticism of his old-fashioned approach; his narrator discusses his own technique.

In chapter 13, Fowles drops his own fictional pretense: "This story I am telling is all imagination. These characters I create never existed outside my own mind. If I have pretended until now to know my characters' minds and innermost thoughts, it is because I am writing in (just as I have assumed some of the vocabulary and 'voice' of) a convention univerally accepted at the time of my story: that the novelist stands next to God. He may not know all, yet he tries to pretend that he does" (95). By exposing his own mechanism, Fowles defies both Victorian preoccupation with the illusion of omniscience and contemporary fixation upon the illusion of detachment.

Bradford Booth defends the Victorian intrusive author on the basis of nineteenth-century reality: "It is charged that he does not maintain a consistent point of view. What matter, if his characters live? It is charged that he sees human nature only from the outside. What matter, if his view be not distorted?"[13] Fowles defends his simultaneous breach of Victorian omniscience and twentieth-century detachment with contemporary philosophy nearer, for example, Joyce's:

> I have disgracefully broken the illusion? No. My characters still exist, and in a reality no less, or no more, real than the one I have just broken. Fiction is woven into all, as a Greek observed some two and a half thousand years ago. I find this new reality (or unreality) more valid; and I would have you share my own sense that I do not fully control these creatures of my mind, any more than you control—however hard you try . . . your children, colleagues, friends, or even yourself. (97)

In essence, Fowles presents a reality akin to such as that of Joyce and Durrell, whose artist characters create their own existence. He says of himself and his fellow novelists, *"We wish to create worlds as real as, but other than the world that is. Or was"* (96). With modern aesthetic reality entirely different from the Victorian kind, Fowles can flout both the nineteenth-century author's pretense to all knowledge and the contemporary one's obsession with impersonal narration.

Fowles is not the first novelist to dispel his own illusion. There are two particularly notable Victorian precedents. A near parallel to his fiction-shattering chapter 13 is Trollope's conclusion to the fifteenth chapter of *Barchester Towers:* "But let the gentle-hearted reader be under no apprehension whatsoever. It is not destined that Eleanor shall marry Mr. Slope or Bertie Stanhope. And here, perhaps, it may be allowed to the novelist to explain his views on a very important point in the art of telling tales. . . . [T]he author and the reader should move along together in full confidence with each other. Let the personages of the drama undergo ever so complete a comedy of errors among themselves."[14] Perhaps the classic breach of illusion in the Victorian novel is the one George Eliot commits in her seventeenth chapter to *Adam Bede,* entitled "In Which the Story Pauses a Little":

> "This Rector of Broxton is little better than a pagan!" I hear one of my readers exclaim. "How much more edifying it would have been if you had made him give Arthur some truly spiritual advice. You might have put into his mouth the most beautiful things—quite as good as reading a sermon." Certainly I could, if I held it the highest vocation of the novelist to represent things as they never have been and never will be. Then, of course, I might refashion life and character entirely after my own liking.[15]

Eliot, like Fowles, devotes her entire chapter to this extended aside. And also like Fowles, she pleads for truth in portraying characters. That argument for reality is one reason Fowles insists that his characters are *free*. In addition to establishing a metaphor for his theology, he is explaining that he cannot violate today's informed ideas of human behavior. But the characters of Trollope, who *has*, perhaps, "disgracefully broken the illusion," are not free in the same sense of realistic probability. In contrast to Fowles, Trollope gains the reader's confidence at the expense of his characters. By conferring metaphorical freedom upon his characters, Fowles gives the opposite impression—seeming to protect his characters from the reader. Earlier parallels to Fowles's declaration of character independence are not unheard of; Fielding, two centuries earlier, protests in *Tom Jones* that he is obliged to divulge certain information himself because he cannot prevail upon any of his characters to speak. To Fielding, the characters are "actors," and unmistakably *his;* their taciturnity is only the author's whimsical humor.

Fowles's often playful intrusions are sometimes as near to devices of Fielding and Sterne as to techniques used by their Victorian successors, but his personal appearance in the novel is more extreme than most inventions of either century. In older traditions, the author sometimes steps into the presence of his *reader,* but Fowles keeps the reader at some distance and actually joins his *characters.* Fielding climbs into a coach with the reader of *Tom Jones,* and Dickens yanks the reader of *The Old Curiosity Shop* away by the hand on a cross-country trip, but neither ever barges into a character's railway compartment.

However much Fowles's showmanship may resemble his capriciously introducing the film of *The Magus* or Hitchcock's popping up in his own cinema, a seriousness underlies this novel's wit and humor. Fowles uses his unconventional techniques purposefully as well as effectively: both his intrusions and his self-limited omniscience are essential to his themes and plot.

By establishing himself candidly as a twentieth-century novelist writing of the preceding century, Fowles assumes the unique vantage point to command the necessary historical view. The narrator needs such perspective to understand Charles's confronting evolution's particular segment which made the twentieth century what it is. Omniscience enables Fowles's narrator to step into

pre-1867 past as well as into twentieth-century present and to
summarize extensive plot material with economy. And the reader
must consider the narrator qualified to make the judgments he
proposes and to depict reliably the events, people, and places he
describes. The omniscient viewpoint further enables Fowles to
expose various characters' thoughts without elaborate technical
ruses. Omniscience would not have been the only way to do so, but
it effectively gives the reader insight to such internal feelings as
Charles's misgivings about involvement with Sarah, Ernestina's
longings and sexual inhibitions, Sam's class-conscious resentments
and schemes, and Mrs. Poulteney's rivalry for a first-class seat in
Paradise. Such mental processes could have been revealed through
an objective omniscience which exposed without comment. But
Fowles's editorial interpretations make possible his Victorian irony,
an important part of the book's humor. This point of view is also the
simplest way to accomplish the job of narration—just as the easiest
way to solve problems and know reality is to believe in the Victorian
God, another irony in Fowles's technique.

Interpolating essay material serves the same kind of double
purpose, making the plot believable while widening the reader's
perspective. Sometimes the essay comprises an entire chapter, in
the manner of Fielding and George Eliot. Chapter 35, an essay on
lower-class sexual freedom and the problem of incest in Thomas
Hardy's life, informs the reader and removes all doubt about why
Sam and Mary appear together at the hay barn. The history of the
gentleman, interpolated within the thirty-seventh chapter, also
informs the reader historically, while explaining Charles's antipathy
to Mr. Freeman's offer of a mercantile career.

Fowles exults in all available Victorian devices to link the epochs
and show history's horizontality: brief authorial comments, foot-
notes, essay materials, and epigraphs foreshadowing the chapters
they precede. By using these conventions as a Victorian novelist
might have, he forcefully connects past and present. To heighten
suspense, he abruptly shifts scene, once leaving Charles peering
over a barn partition for an entire chapter. Except in Sarah's case,
he reveals character through direct narration. He sprinkles his text
with documents, stories-within-stories, and personal letters: the
Freeman attorneys' legal paper, Grogan's case histories, Ernestina's
sentimental novel, the eighteenth-century account of a London
brothel, and written correspondence between Charles and other

characters—to mention several. The narrator's intrusions often control the reader's sympathy for characters: the term "catatonia of convention" increases one's distance from the jilted Tina; and the comment on Charles's first poem, "to get the taste of that from your mouth," moves the focus away from his character's aching heart. Fowles's sometimes clinically probing his characters' minds is another way of keeping the reader's sympathy at proper distance.

But Sarah is the novel's one thoroughly modern character, and Fowles strengthens her contemporary quality, along with her mystery, by making her the only one whose mind he will not enter. In the Darwinian sense, she is the cultural "missing link" between the centuries—more modern than Victorian. By voluntarily limiting his Victorian omniscience in her case alone, Fowles adds another dimension to the evolution theme. His other restriction of Victorian narrative technique—his demurral over authorial omnipotence (95–97)—further links by showing the evolution of the novelist's role, especially as it applies to man's evolving concept of a god. The narrator's appearing as character and the reader's choosing between multiple endings emphasize concepts of literary, theological, and social evolution.

V *The Novelist as Character*

The novelist enters his book in three appearances—first like an owl who becomes human beneath Sarah's window. And he gives the novel three endings—the first of which damns Charles to a lifetime of reading that maddening verse Ernestina has stitched on his watch pocket, then more justly, plummets Mrs. Poulteney into Tartarus. But that tongue-in-cheek denouement is only how Charles dreams things *might* have turned out, with each winding of his watch reminding him indeed of love: the love he had missed. The last two endings—one Victorian, the other contemporary—are the ones which determine the book's final impact, just as do the narrator's diverse personae on his two more blatant trips into the novel.

When the narrator first intrudes upon Charles's railway compartment, he is incognito as the archetypal Victorian novelist. Like Thackeray, he is "prophet-bearded," the bullying "tabernacle" preacher, his top hat squared, "aggressively secure," with the look of an omnipotent god—"if there were such an absurd thing"—who wonders of his character, "Now could I use you? Now what could I do with you?" But his habit and demeanor are only a disguise; he is still the contemporary novelist, who is really wondering what the devil he is to do with Charles in a novel whose Victorian conventions forbid an open, inconclusive, ending[16] and whose contemporary views preclude "fixing the fight" (405). Having vowed to take neither Charles's nor Sarah's side, he decides upon two endings to their story and is caught tossing a florin to determine which will be the last, and therefore the more powerful.

When the narrator at last reappears to effect that final ending, his new disguise clarifies why the toss has gone to the contemporary, open, ending. No longer done up as the preaching, Victorian, omnipotent-god novelist, he is now the successful novelist-impresario (notorious "fixers" of their dramatic enterprises, despite their respectable pose). He, "as he would put it, has got himself in *as he really is*. I shall not labor the implication that he was previously got in as he really wasn't" (461). Now he has "an almost proprietary air," dandified clothes, a "foppish and Frenchified" beard, the look of a "tycoon." Contrary to protests of *nouveau roman* stylists, the modern novelist is no less in control of his own fiction than the Victorian who acknowledged his omniscience: "In this he has not changed: he very evidently regards the world as his to possess and use as he likes." As the contemporary novelist carried grandly into his unique, part-Victorian novel, the dandified narrator is making his point about the evolution of both theology and literary technique: the Victorian novelist, in the context of Victorian reality, could assume the omniscience which his age attributed to God; but the contemporary novelist, in the context of twentieth-century reality, must maintain the illusion of nonintervention, in this age which no longer believes in a controlling deity. But both Victorian and modern authors have always controlled their own fiction, as Fowles's contemporary impresario-novelist demonstrates. Although he refuses the role of intervening god, he accepts the role of novelist with all of its dramatic manipulations. The Victorian novelist might have tossed a coin, but the contemporary writer can control his novel's *time*. And this one does—thus giving the existential perspective on events which themselves cannot be controlled, i.e., changed. It is *his* florin (a two-headed one, perhaps) which has determined the final ending; now it is *his* watch (a Breguet, the finest) which effaces the previous quarter hour to make way for that final and contemporary ending.

VI   *The Endings: Victorian and Modern*

From its ancient beginnings in magic, then religious, ritual and drama, fiction was characterized by closed endings: victories, sacred marriages, births, and deaths. If the hero lost, his defeat grew out of some tragic flaw—some misunderstanding with the gods which alienated their affections. If he won, his victory came from the gods as a reward for his virtue. For centuries, fiction's closed endings assured the accomplishment of divine justice—however miraculous and improbable the *deus ex machina* necessary to bring it about. Even well into the Victorian Age, the novel's closed ending remained a function of divine intervention—although often, at this stage, a sort of secularized version in which the hero was rewarded with the girl and the wealth. However materialistically, the novelist-god gave the protagonist justice—at least until Dickens dropped Stephen Blackpool down a mineshaft and Hardy's heroes began to suffer from their author's deterministic views.

Except for such writers as Hardy and the later Dickens, the novelist in the epoch of the decreeing Victorian god had no qualms about intervening in his story to effect the closed ending of his choice. And to make his ending happen, the novelist frequently relied upon the most improbable of coincidences. Infants abandoned in railway stations miraculously reappeared years later to claim inheritances; long-lost relatives were reunited across continents and oceans; and heroes were catapulted from poverty to wealth by convergences of the most unlikely circumstances. Although today's novel usually shuns even the barely coincidental, the Victorian novel's closed endings often defied all natural law and mathematical probability. And Lalage, the child whose birth to Charles and Sarah provides the denouement for the first, the closed, ending, is one of those improbable Victorian devices.

Lalage is the conventional *deus ex machina*—or more accurately *dea ex uno coito*—whose birth is believable enough in a Victorian context. But the modern reader who knows his physiology would, however willing, require a block-and-tackle to suspend disbelief. Although it is certainly *possible* that Sarah might have conceived from a single union, the odds against that eventuality are better than five-to-one, even under the best of conditions. The conditions, however, are not optimum. The brief consummation of Charles and Sarah may be literature's definitive premature climax: its ninety seconds include not only Charles's feverish undressing but also his travel time—for two-and-a-half round trips between sitting room and bedroom.[17] Charles attributes the happy ending to "God's hands." And rightly so, since biological probability weighs against Lalage's birth, which might have been prevented by variations in ovulation, spermatogenesis, sperm motility, and other factors—not the least of which is genetic mutation, the evolutionary process mentioned in the final chapter's first epigram: "Evolution is simply the process by which chance ['hazard', in British usage] (the random mutations in the nucleic acid helix caused by natural radiation [gamma-ray particles]) cooperates with natural law to create living forms better and better adapted to survive."

Fowles instructs the reader, "But what you must not think is that this is a less plausible ending to their story. For I have returned, albeit deviously, to my original principle: that there is no intervening god beyond whatever can be seen, in that way, in the first epigraph to this chapter; thus only life as we have, within our hazard-given abilities, made it ourselves, life as Marx defined it—*the actions of men* (and of women) *in pursuit of their ends.*" (466).

Not only is this final ending not less plausible, it is by far the more probable—biologically, as well as psychologically. For, in protesting that his impresario-novelist is "as minimal, in fact, as a gamma-ray particle," Fowles links him to the Gardner epigraph and shows him to intervene as *chance, hazard*—natural radiation, the evolutionary agent which might have inhibited Lalage's birth.[18]

The final ending is thus true to Fowles's biological view. But it is also true to his sense of mystery, for even biology cannot explain it completely. Even in this final ending, there is an unidentified child. Lalage, perhaps? We shall never know.

But this thoroughly contemporary final ending is the one supported by the vast thematic network which has woven into the novel the concepts of man's isolation and his survival through the centuries by *evolving*. Finally, even the reader himself must choose whether to evolve: if he takes the final ending, he has chosen evolution. But if he accepts the happy ending, he must accept along with it its Victorian intervening God, its biological and psychological improbability, its heavy-handed rendering, and its wretched musical accompaniment—the "untalented lady" attempting a Chopin mazurka.

VII *Biological and Social Evolution*

Fowles considers man's happiness an outgrowth of knowing that he has survived—and man's survival a feat only possible by evolving. But to evolve, survive, and be happy, man must also suffer the unhappiness brought on by chance, by the hazard essential to the evolutionary process: "The purpose of Hazard is to force us, and the rest of matter, to evolve. It is only by evolving that we, in a process that is evolving, can continue to survive. The purpose of *human* evolution is therefore to recognize this: that we must evolve to exist" (A, 42).

Since man, despite his talk of progress, is highly resistant to change, and since Fowles is particularly aware of constant adaptation as a requisite of existence, evolution is at the base of his biological view. The sort of human evolving which concerns Fowles most is psychological rather than physiological; it is the rational, conscious process that takes place when a person recognizes the alternatives from which he must choose if he is to survive. Darwin's ideas of natural selection and survival of the fittest are at the core of Fowles's philosophy, and since man is the rational animal, the quality of fitness for him is intelligence—with its corollary quality of kindness, since it is difficult for a truly intelligent man to be unkind.

Charles, fortunately, has both qualities and so is able to undergo the evolution necessary for survival. His ordeal is not pleasant or easy. Nor does he understand much of what is happening to him. And Sarah, although she guides him into the agonizing process that leads eventually to freedom for them both, is not necessarily aware, in a rational sense, of what her proceedings are effecting. It is appropriate here to consider Jung's psychology of the female mind, since it explains why Sarah embraces the role of outcast and leads Charles to his eventual freedom by the same route. Unlike rationally directed men, Jung says, women are motivated by emotions geared toward a specific end, although the end is often beyond their recognition as they work toward it. The concept is something like "woman's intuition," and it is not like male motivation through the unconscious mind, "for her moods and emotions do not come to her directly from the unconscious, but are peculiar to her feminine nature. They are therefore never naive, but mixed with unacknowledged purpose."[19] Even to such a scholarly Victorian male as Dr. Grogan, Sarah's motives appear symptomatic of hysteria,[20] but it eventually becomes evident that her feelings are instead mingled with "unacknowledged purpose." Polonius would have understood.

Sarah's assuming the role of fallen woman not only exempts her from the usual restrictions of sex and class; it also casts her in the particular anima role of sensual seductress, an image extremely attractive to Charles's unconscious mind. Sarah's involving him in her own fate by tempting him to freedom is typical of what Jung considers the sexual pattern of woman's machinations: "By maintaining a passive attitude with an invisible purpose in the background, she aids a man towards his realization, and in that way holds him. At the same time she weaves a web of fate for herself, because whoever digs a pit for others falls himself therin."[21] Jung does not mention that the first woman to carry out that sexual pattern of leading a man into this sort of mutual fate was, of course, Eve. Like that ancestral seductress, Sarah, in "an English Garden of Eden," tempts Charles to self-knowledge, then is cast out along with him when he accepts her temptation.

The novel's symbols center around the fall of man—his gaining knowledge while losing a paradise of ignorance. In the green and Edenic Undercliff, though Charles seeks an extinct species, he discovers a new one instead: Sarah, who leads him through knowledge to become a new species himself. The wildness of the Undercliff, in absolute contrast to the hothouse where he proposes to civilized Ernestina, matches Sarah's natural wildness. When she offers him the tests, with her implication of much more, she is Eve offering the forbidden fruit; she *tests* his fitness to survive; she *tests* his manhood. She offers him evolution, and, true to Fowles's naturalistic view, Charles's chance to evolve comes largely through a biological impulse—his sexuality. Even the name and shape of the tests resemble those of testes, though the names stem from different Latin roots. In addition, the tests represent a fossilized state which might await Charles. Those ancient echinoderms are long extinct; their descendants, the sand dollars, have learned to survive— perhaps by presenting a lower profile. Evolutionists regard the sea urchins as man's remote ancestors—one particular parallel which Fowles says he intended. And it is largely by studying echinoderms that scientists have advanced their knowledge of fertilization as well as of genetic mutation—evolution's biological process.

In the context of social evolution, Charles begins with a misconception of his own place in Darwin's universe. He considers himself, an educated young gentleman, naturally selected for survival, little suspecting that his class is marked instead for extinction. In British society, it is the Sams and the Mr. Freemans who will survive; even the Grogans will be no more. Although Charles fancies himself a disciple of Darwin, he misunderstands his own position in Darwin's theories. Darwin had finally disposed of belief in an anthropocentric universe and in that already moribund hierarchy of existence which had ranked man next to the angels. Yet Charles, no doubt like many of his peers, interprets the new theories in an anthropocentric way which is sociocentric and egocentric as well:

> Charles called himself a Darwinist, and yet he had not really understood Darwin. . . . [H]e saw in the [rock] strata an immensely reassuring orderliness in existence. He might perhaps have seen a very contemporary social symbolism in the way those gray-blue ledges were crumbling; but what he did see was a kind of edificiality of time, in which inexorable laws (therefore beneficently divine, for who could argue that order was not the highest human good?) very conveniently arranged themselves for the survival of the fittest and best, *exemplia gratia* Charles Smithson, this fine spring day, alone, eager and inquiring, understanding, accepting, noting and grateful. (49)

Sarah's unmistakable offer finally destroys all this complacency for Charles. She becomes in his mind the embodiment of all that is alluring and exciting in existence, and the prospect of Ernestina and the Freeman department store for a lifetime looks increasingly like the matrix which will encase him in stone. Leaving his meeting with Ernestina's father, Charles at last feels the onset of extinction. Miserable and outcast, "he felt that the enormous apparatus rank required a gentleman to erect around himself was like the massive armor that had been the death warrant of so many ancient saurian species. His step slowed at this image of a superseded monster. He actually stopped, poor living fossil, as the brisker and fitter forms of life jostled busily before him, like pond amoeba under a microscope . . ." (290). Charles feels trapped by conventions of rank and economics, and he is uncomfortably aware of the natural freedom among the lower classes—particularly their uninhibited sexuality. Unconsciously associating freedom with sexuality is his important attraction to Sarah. He is taunted by low-class songs like "Why don'cher com 'ome, Lord Marmaduke," by the obvious sexual freedom of Sam and Mary, by his remembrances of sexual encounters outside England. And Sarah's smile is more than he can ultimately resist.

Had he resisted—because of conforming to social convention—he would have been resisting the act of evolution. In so doing, he would have been giving himself up to extinction along with the gentlemanly class, failing to extricate himself from the matrimonial, economic, social entrapment that would petrify his freedom and therefore his existence. In the first, imagined, ending to the story, Charles leaves Sarah and her temptation behind, remaining one of those who fail to survive. She represents "all his lost possibilities, his extinct freedoms, his never-to-be-taken journeys." He fancies himself "one more ammonite caught in the vast movements of history, stranded now for eternity, a potential turned to a fossil" (333). If that destiny had really been his, instead of being a probability Charles had dreamed true, his failure would have been denying his natural instinct for freedom, an impulse strongly linked to human sexuality.

Sarah's feelings for Charles are intensely sexual, as his are for her. Although Ernestina's "I must not" prohibits even *thoughts* of sex, Sarah's entire approach to Charles is sexual—and it is more than a ploy for freedom; it is her honestly wanting Charles, much as she had presumably desired the French lieutenant. She is no longer deceiving Charles when she admits seducing him because she has thought of her own happiness; and in sending him away, she is making a sacrifice for him. She does not say that she cannot marry him—but that he cannot marry *her*, and she apparently thinks that he will return to Ernestina. "You have given me the consolation of believing that in another world, another age, another life, I might have been your wife. . . . There is one thing in which I have not deceived you. I loved you . . . I think from the moment I saw you" (355). Neither is Sarah deceiving Charles when she pleads that she cannot explain her own action. But her suggesting her own sociosexual envy is illuminated by Jung's comment on women who remain single and compete with wives: "the married women must be driven out; not as a rule by open and forcible means, but by that quiet and obstinate wish, that works as we all know magically, like the fixed eye of the snake. This has always been the way of woman."[22] But envy is hardly Sarah's only motive. She is what Jung considers the new woman whose masculine aggressiveness brings her near facultative homosexuality (hence her protective intimacy with the maid Millie) and also intensifies her need for intimacy with the male.[23] Despite her need, Sarah tries to send Charles back to Ernestina.

Sarah rejects Charles initially out of self-sacrifice—the sort of generosity assertive women often show the men they love. Jung praises the courage and capacity for self-sacrifice in women like Sarah.[24] But in another sense, Sarah's discouraging Charles and fleeing is as much self-serving as self-sacrificial; she seems to realize, especially after their brief consummation, that an alliance with Charles would be impossible as long as he continues to marinate himself in guilt. She could hardly foresee the epiphany which strikes him when he has left her to cry alone.

In the deserted church, Charles's realization brings him to the choice which even Sarah may never have expected of him. He accepts Christ's uncrucifixion and Sarah's unmartyrdom at the same time. He keeps seeing Sarah's tearstained face instead of Christ's, and he weeps because he knows that his prayer goes unheard. When he at last sees the Savior as a kindly and reasoning friend, Jesus leads Charles to accept His humanity and life—not His godliness and martyrdom. Charles also recognizes that Sarah is no martyr either, that she is instead a woman who loves him. In choosing her, he is still, however, choosing ostracism for himself and deserting all that his epoch and class hold sacred. Escape, says the image of Christ, is not a single act but one which he will have to renew constantly: "Each day, Charles, each hour, it has to be taken again. Each minute the nail waits to be hammered in. You know your choice. You stay in prison, what your time calls duty, honor, self-respect, and you are comfortably safe. Or you are free and crucified. Your only companions the stones, the thorns, the turning backs; the silence of cities, and their hate" (362). Despite the ignominy and pain of his decision, Charles continues to renew it even when he begins to lose hope of finding Sarah. Plunged into the existential void, he grows stronger during his two years of lonely wandering. At last, when he confronts her again (and here I consider only the final ending, since the Lalage denouement is provided by divine coincidence), his refusal to accept her implied offer of a relationship on her terms is evidence of the self-sufficiency which he has developed, for he has begun "to realize that life, however advantageously Sarah may in some ways seem to fit the role of Sphinx, is not a symbol, is not one riddle and one failure to guess it . . ." (467).[25] Through his own lonely suffering, Charles has learned what Sarah's has taught her: the way to exist within the hazard of the existential void, through reliance upon self-awareness.

The final chapter's first epigram establishes God as the interaction of hazard with natural law. This largely biological concept of determinism is, although more positive, akin to Thomas Hardy's philosophy of Immanent Will. Hardy, who admired Darwin enough to attend his funeral, broods over this entire novel, and his own image of "purblind doomsters" governing man's destiny is similar to Fowles's "hazard-given abilities." But Fowles surpasses Hardy's deterministic view by showing how to live under such an uncertain scheme of existence.

Although Sarah has given Charles his freedom, she has done so partly because she values *hers*. As Fowles says, she has always been guided by *acting what she knows*—that principle of Matthew Arnold's in the final chapter's second epigram. At last Charles has learned the same principle. When he finally returns her gift, he is acting on his own knowledge that Sarah's love would only possess him. In gaining the *self*-awareness and *self*-sufficiency that characterize the existential consciousness, both characters have also embraced something of the *selfishness* (not entirely in the word's pejorative sense) that accompanies acting what one knows. This side-effect of the existential awareness, far more advanced in Sarah's case, is the twentieth century's greatest barrier to love. What has happened to Sarah's ability to be simultaneously loving and independent is a preview of today's conflict between feeling and will. That conflict within Sarah is the reason that Charles's accepting her implied offer of a relationship would be hurting her most, as he sees that she is suddenly frightened to realize.

Though the existential awareness has taken from Charles the Victorian blind adherence to duty, honor, and self-respect, it has mercifully left him the Victorian "ability to give that was also an inability to compromise"—the facility which, as the narrator says, is his true superiority to Sarah. That uncompromising capacity to give is also the true superiority of the Victorian age to our own. In his seventeenth century, John Donne wrote that "no man is an island"; in Charles Smithson's epoch, Matthew Arnold's "To Marguerite" reversed Donne's metaphor to say that *every* man is enisled. It is fitting that John Fowles, in the twentieth century, ends his unique novel with Arnold's lines. In our personal insularity, we species of today, evolved from predecessors such as Charles and Sarah, scoff at our Victorian ancestors' sentimentality—antiquated notions, outmoded novel forms. But unfortunately, like Sarah, most of us have evolved so fiercely in pursuing our ends and preserving our *selves* that we have devalued our feelings along with our Victorian misconceptions. This tragic loss is part of the existential dilemma which confronts Sarah and Charles, long before that puzzle of the will ever got its name.

CHAPTER 5

The Ebony Tower

I *Variations*

IN the section of *The Ebony Tower* called "A Personal Note," John Fowles explains that the book's working title, *Variations*, referred to both themes and narrative techniques. The stories in this collection, as he says, are variations in both senses. Technically they continue his practice of varying narrative method from story to story. Thematically, these variations amplify ideas prominent in his other works. Moreover, the book's title novella, its translated Celtic romance, and its three short stories share the common theme of art and life, important in all of Fowles's books.

The hero of *The Magus* initially confuses art with life, form with content, style with meaning. *The Collector* shows the tragic effect of social imbalance upon both people and art. And *The French Lieutenant's Woman* links literary and cultural evolution. Similarly, the title story of *The Ebony Tower* relates artistic movements to human values. Its medieval companion story, the Celtic romance *Eliduc,* exposes cultural pretenses which were largely stylistic. "Poor Koko" forces confrontation between stylistic representatives of society's verbal and nonverbal extremes. "The Enigma" concerns fiction and real mystery. And "The Cloud" links fiction to the inexorability of things, while contrasting the literary word with the self-serving cliché—a mindless force which stifles both art and life. Each of these stories does far more; I summarize only their ways of relating aesthetic sensibility to human behavior. Like man's life, his art can be, among other things, a refuge, a mask, an obsession, a delusion, a profession, a social barrier, a selfish device, a reflection of thought, a style of civilization, an enlightenment, and a fulfilling act of natural creativity. As in Fowles's earlier fiction, his stories in *The Ebony Tower* present these themes, with a network of others, in several variations.

116

II   *The Ebony Tower, the Quest, and the Style*

The eight-century-old epigram to Fowles's novella describes the archetypal quest of the knight, who, often leaving a lover behind, reaches some mysterious master's castle and gains entry against dubious odds:

> And through forests long and wide
> Through landscapes strange and savage
> And passing through many treacherous trails
> And many a peril and many a trial
> Until he came straightway to the path.
>
> (Chrétien de Troyes, *Yvain*)

Once inside the castle, the knight usually becomes somehow involved with at least one nubile damsel—more often *two*—rarely more. Of the customary two, one is distant and desirable, the other accessible and less attractive—occasionally not pretty at all but haggish instead. Sometimes the hag is transformed; sometimes the two maidens prove to be one; but the hero usually discovers to his eventual surprise that the master is not as mysterious, nor the princess as distant, as he had supposed. Almost inevitably, she at last becomes available—whether he decides to keep her or not.

The Germanic obsession with conquering lands and the Byzantine obsession with conquering souls gave the medieval romance most of its dragons and battles, crusades and pious sentiments. But the Celtic British, with their wilder and deeper imagination, provided most of its magicians, fairies, and elves, along with a company of its gnomes, goblins, and giants. In addition, the Celtic influence helped expose several even stranger monsters, not the least of which was the conflict between chivalry's female-oriented tradition of courtly love and its male-dominated compulsion to adventure and violence. Centuries of males have flown to war and arms while protesting that they could not love their women so much, loved they not honor more. Masculine power politics still threatens modern mankind. It is no wonder that Fowles, in his "Personal Note," calls the Watergate tragedy more cultural than political, nor that he links its hidden demons with the opposition of sexual adventure to mutual trust between lovers. This discord underlies both the modern story "The Ebony Tower" and the medieval romance *Eliduc*—appropriately, because from medieval times to our own, many a story, both fictional and real, has left its princess weeping.

But as wiser writers have always shown, romantic impulses send man to his greatest happinesses as well as his deepest sorrows, and stifling his quests after mystery would also smother his nobility and creativity. Modern man, subduing his emotions after the romantic excess of World War II, has weakened his power to love while trying to control his hatred. Our century's reaction against extreme *feeling*—both political and aesthetic—has tipped the stylistic balance of both art and society in favor of *logic*—often a cold and myopic style of it.

In today's emotion-fearing epoch, the precise young men of Watergate, reacting against past totalitarian horrors, could logically and unemotionally apply the very methods that began those horrors, and then could justify their chilling logic with clichés that fixed human events "at that point in time." In this euphemistic age when wars are no longer "fought" but "escalated" and when pilots remote in air-conditioned cockpits call slaughter "pacification," our culture has partially expurgated precision in meaning while imposing excessive precision in form. The result is an erosion of specificity, both linguistic and artistic. The imprisonment of image which has "liberated" speech and art, and the imprisonment of feeling which has "liberated" sex, both epitomize the current trend toward abstraction—today's stylistic flight from the past's emotional excess. But Hitler, whose romantic ghost we flee, could icily describe genocide with the abstraction "final solution" and *stylize* his terror away from reality—quite as the proponents of chivalry, in pursuit of order, could *stylize* away their own inconsistencies. In her twelfth century, Marie de France saw through the pretenses of the chivalric style—just as Fowles, in his own twentieth century, sees through the pretenses of abstraction.

Fowles sets his title novella against these two polar extremes: the romantic and the abstract views of reality. But his own avowed belief is in the balance of counterpoles, and his naturalistic view, which depends upon *the living reality*, would place that reality near the balancing point. A deeper conflict of the story is the tension between balance and extremisms. But *living reality* is never the elusive balance itself, but rather cycles of counteraction between opposites. With Fowles's belief in hazard and mystery, fixing absolute equilibrium is impossible and illusory; Fowles's reality is *the quest itself*—man's search for balance somewhere amid nature's extremes, through her vast forests, which conceal both dangers and delights.

III   The Ebony Tower

When young David Williams, a British abstract artist and critic, arrives at the French forest domain of Henry Breasley, a seventy-seven-year-old expatriate British painter, he approaches in an aura of mystery that might have greeted a knight arriving before the castle perilous. The old farmhouse first appears deserted, as had Bourani in *The Magus*, and as had the mysterious *domaine* in *Le Grand Meaulnes*. But, as the heroes of the other two novels discover, David finds entry easy: the deceptive padlock would have given at his pull. Old Breasley's loose gate, like Conchis's broken fence, suggests that awareness is more accessible to the hero than it seems.

David, writing the introduction to a book of Breasley's paintings, is seeking the roots of the old man's art, influences of other artists and traditions. Although David reasons that Breasley, having granted the interview, must consider his previous criticism on the right trail, David is apprehensive at the old man's formidable reputation—rumors of petulance and blatant lechery. He finds the latter gossip apparently confirmed by the presence of Diana and Anne, two English girls Breasley has dubbed, respectively, the Mouse and the Freak. Contemporary versions of the medieval castle's two damsels, the Mouse, a talented art student, is initially distant and mysteriously attractive; the Freak, a skinny refugee from the drug scene, is the "absurd sex doll" with an air of easy availability. One is ideal, the other reality. Like a twentieth-century knight, David must weather something of an ordeal before discovering part of the mystery behind Breasley, the castle's master. Also like many a knight, before his trial's end, he finds himself torn between Diana, the suddenly available princess, and Beth, the wife he has left behind. If the story were a medieval romance, it might have ended with some pompous resolution. But instead, set in 1973, the tale is contemporary, and Fowles rejects the option of an absolute conclusion. Its ending, like that final one in *The French Lieutenant's Woman*, is true to the modern age, open and incompletely resolved. Like many a twentieth-century hero, David himself is left in a state of irresolution, having barely "survived," though a wiser man.

Like the medieval castle's inscrutable host, Breasley guards his secrets carefully, initially even pretending ignorance of well-known artists and technical terms. But he acknowledges admiring the

French cubist Georges Braque, a close friend during Breasley's days in Paris. Although he scoffs at Braque's "synthetic cubist nonsense," Breasley has financed his own estate, Coëtminais, with the proceeds from a Braque painting. His only remaining Braque hangs prominently over his bed, an ironic location, since Breasley disparages abstract art's asexuality along with its theoretical qualities. Arguing hotly, he likens reality to the female genitals and "all that goes with them." When David replies that abstract art is concerned with the mind instead, Breasley directly attacks his sexuality, even questioning his wife's happiness.

The exchange prominently links abstraction to war and politics as well. Having termed the movement art's greatest betrayal, Breasley goes on to call it the "Triumph of the bloody eunuch." David counters with, "At least better than the triumph of the bloody dictator?" The old painter answers, "Balls. Spunk. Any spunk. Even Hitler's spunk. Or nothing."[1] David, representing the deepest fear beneath today's tendency toward abstraction, is speaking for its reaction against fascism, the age's greatest romantic extreme. But Breasley, though patently lacking verbal skill to express his insight, sees both sides of Hitler's relationship to abstract art. Attacking the idea of turning the other cheek (submission he compares to anal intercourse), Breasley continues, "Same old story. Sit on the bloody English fence. Vote for Adolf." Too much wine has intensified Breasley's difficulty with words, and neither David nor Diana understands how well the old man knows the two extremes at issue. She reprimands him with, "Henry, you can't stop totalitarian ideas by totalitarian methods. That way you only help breed them" (45). Though Breasley had been a "characteristically militant pacifist" during World War I, he had served as medical orderly in the Spanish Civil War; his fellow British had shunned the truth of his war drawings until they too faced Hitler.

Before his involvement in war, Breasley had spent a period in what Fowles calls the "no-man's-land between surrealism and communism"—a "queasy" position because of Russia's artistic retreat to socialist realism. But the Spanish Civil War had taught him what his countrymen failed to realize until later: "Like most artists, Breasley had been well ahead of the politicians. To the British the 1942 exhibition suddenly made sense; they too had learned what war was about, of the bitter folly of giving the benefit of the doubt to international fascism" (11). Breasley, despite his verbal inability, is still ahead of the politicians, and ahead of any style of art or life which devalues feeling. He dismisses the painting *Guernica*, Picasso's abstraction of that Basque city's destruction in 1937 by Franco's German bombers, as a "good gravestone" which allows a show of "fine feelings" by those who ignored the atrocity when it happened. With Franco still in power after an amazing thirty-six years, Breasley has good reason to rail at those who abstract their own feelings to condone such a dictator. Henry Breasley is not simply attacking abstract art; he is attacking the style, both aesthetic and political, which can allow itself to die, either metaphorically or literally, for lack of feeling. Breasley's own metaphor for both abstract life style and abstract art style is "The Ebony Tower"— looming as more sinister, more coldly dark and deathlike than the bright Ivory Tower into which more romantically inclined artists had fled ills of earlier ages. In departing from reality through an unfeeling life and an emotionless art, the age of the Ebony Tower threatens life—including its own moribund one—by fearing both to create life and to live it. Only extremists with unchecked feeling can rule such an unfeeling culture. The Hitlers and Francos and, potentially, the Nixons take over while unemotional men calmly do their bidding. Breasley's fear of such abandonment of feeling is his reason for saying, "Better the bloody bomb than Jackson Bollock." He knows the danger in sacrificing feeling to abstraction like Pollock's random paint-splattering, an aesthetic reflection of emotionless murdering on order. Precursors of such men as the Nazis unfeelingly use oppressive defenses against threats of oppression, as the Nixon administration did. Old Breasley shudders at his nightmare visions of the Ebony Tower, and hanged corpses in Pisanello's *St. George and the Princess* reinforce his childhood terror at Foxe's *Book of Martyrs*. The Foxe woodcuts show expressionless mobs calmly torturing Protestants to death under Bloody Mary's Catholic reign. Breasley knows the horror that follows man's subordinating human feeling to abstract ideas such as Catholicism, Nazism, Cubism, Communism, or Democracy.

The Ebony Tower holds an even more personal fear for Henry Breasley. His own art reflects the naturalism of Pisanello, the fifteenth-century Veronese painter. But Breasley's last two paintings are nearer the spirit of Pisanello's Florentine contemporary Paolo Uccello, who wasted his art and life experimenting with perspective. *Night Hunt,* Uccello's most natural painting, has influenced both Breasley's *Moon Hunt* and his current work *Kermesse,* which grows continually more ominous. Pisanello had kept nature in his art despite having to serve the Byzantine state as medalist. But Uccello, victimized by the Ebony Tower's quattrocento counterpart, had let style usurp feeling; his successor Sandro Botticelli was soon serving on a hanging committee.[2] Breasley, sensing his own kinship to Uccello, has reason to be tormented by specters of both the hanged men and the Ebony Tower. And since Uccello had apparently neglected his wife's affections in search of perspective, the Braque over Breasley's bed becomes an even greater irony.

Diana might have become a sort of muse to David as she is to Breasley, but she and David are as emotionally controlled as their abstract art is. He admires her cool honesty; she even wears "safe" autumnal colors. Characteristic of the contemporary flight from emotion, their reserve makes life less risky. Even when Diana offers the Edenic apple, it is carefully peeled, and David and Breasley get only a quarter each. She becomes less antiseptic, however, when she leaves the role of mouse-muse[3] for that of dragon-weasel.

The mouse is an ancient female sex symbol, the muse woman's creative aspect. But dragons and weasels, the largest and smallest of slinky predators, have suffered a bad press in symbolism. The dragon's ill temper and bad breath have cast it as threatening evil; the weasel's shape and smell have given it the shady reputation of seductress.[4] Fowles links the weasel in *Eliduc* to the one in his own story, but neither weasel's human counterpart is very guilty. Guilliadun had begun in innocence, and Diana at last preserves David's by locking her door. Despite her also having been "the girl cast as dragon," David remorsefully sees his marital fidelity as weakness, Breasley's loose behavior as creative courage: "He sinned out of need and instinct; David did not, out of fear" (108). Bitterly regretting his lost opportunity, David is temporarily ashamed of being "obsessed with means, not ends." He has not yet recalled Breasley's references to Hitler, who had the opposite obsession. Furious at art's amorality, David equates his own moderation with mediocrity. "Coët had remorselessly demonstrated what he was born, still was, and always would be: a decent man and eternal also-ran" (113).

But David's moral dilemma may have taught him more than he first perceives. Though art is amoral, life is not. David had begun his quest busily recording nature in abstract line and tone, but he has now been compelled to face reality. As the narrator had said, "No amount of reading and intelligent deduction could supplant the direct experience" (4). He has had to confront his own *nature,* seeking and sexual, beyond aesthetic or social theory. Diana had called ideas "inherently dangerous because they deny human facts. The only answer to fascism is the human fact" (46). David is brought up sharply against his own human fact, and despite his temporary inability to extricate his life from his art, decency need not make him a failure. Old Breasley's intemperate life has left him a some- what pathetic figure, tongue-tied and fearful of both extremes: the Ebony Tower's sterility and romanticism's potential inhumanity. Although David thinks himself cowardly, his sexual hesitation had grown out of respect for his marriage—another *human fact*.

We in the Ebony Tower's shadow cannot ignore the excesses of feeling which caused our epoch to erect it; nor can we scoff at the courtly love tradition, a medieval attempt to govern feeling. We cannot "cut the root" completely, as Braque had contended, if we recognize both yesterday's courtly love and today's abstraction as imperfect but basically humanitarian styles. As Fowles observes, "*amour courtois* was a desperately needed attempt to bring more civilization (more female intelligence) into a brutal society, and all civilization is based on agreed codes and symbols of mutual trust" (122). Those codes and symbols, in art or society, become useless or dangerous only when they grow to contradict the *human fact*. Through the ages, the best art, like that of Marie de France, Pisanello, and John Fowles, has revealed those contradictions.

IV   "*Poor Koko*"

"Poor Koko" displays another symptom of abstraction. The story shows all that has gone wrong in today's linguistic excesses: the tendency to relinquish precision of language, to rely upon euphemisms, to let jargon stand in place of sense, and to polarize mankind into those who manage words and those who distrust them. Fowles's narrator, who begins as something of a linguistic manipulator, confronts one of the verbally deprived, and his re- counting shows how the incident has made him wield his literacy more kindly.

The narrator, a literary critic, is at the upper limit of today's verbal hierarchy, concealing physical timidity beneath snobbish discourse. Puny and myopic, he has taken up the pen, but the cultural near-tragedy that haunts this story is that the pen *really is* mightier than the sword and that, in a negligent hand, it can destroy by ignoring as well as by attacking.

Although this feeble narrator provides his creator open season on the critics, Fowles's shots are sporting ones. The narrator's better nature outweighs his worse. Although he dislikes Fowles's kindred spirit Thomas Hardy, he is writing a biography of Thomas Love Peacock, whom Fowles praises as England's most neglected novelist. This story's setting and plot resemble those of a Peacock novel, with a characteristic encounter in an isolated spot; and the narrator-critic likes Peacock's stand against "all that was not humane, intelligent, and balanced" (148). As he writes this account, the narrator carefully and honestly admits his old faults as a literary critic and as a responsible person as well; he is now more humane, intelligent, and balanced than he had been before the events of his story. He redeems himself with his move toward reconciling the cultural divorce of language from experience. And he does so in a way which intrinsically reunites the two by using them both: he learns from his experience as victim, then interprets that experience through language, both retrospectively and introspectively.

The little critic expects the burglar, who is "doing" the Dorset summer cottage his friends have lent him, to be less intelligent than he proves to be. The older man notices that his own fearful hesitation to act disgusts the young intruder, whose first question of him is, "Why you so shit scared, man?" (155). Along with the burglar's clichés and fragmentary sentences, the narrator remembers his relative kindness, as well as his respect for people despite his disrespect for their wealth and property. Characteristically English in the antiestablishment manner Fowles elsewhere associates with Robin Hood, the young rebel refuses to "do" museums, out of reverence for their availability to everyone. He carefully preys only upon the well-to-do, whose greed he resents. Although his Marxist platitudes are a flimsy justification for burglary, he is not excessively greedy himself, returning ten percent of his victim's money and passing up dangerously conspicuous valuables. Even approaching his apparently spiteful act of burning the critic's Peacock papers, he continues to be kind, and he had not hesitated to express his own fear at their first encounter.

Though of the nonverbal generation, the intruder scorns the words he seeks. Among his favorite books are Joseph Conrad's sea stories—understandably, in view of their glorifying the ability to act, to immerse oneself in "the destructive element." Conrad's taciturn men often act with decision: Captain MacWhirr, though unable to converse beyond necessity, saves the *Nan Shan* and her more expressive but less decisive officers; and Singleton, Conrad's patriarchal old helmsman who speaks his monosyllables rarely, carefully steers the *Narcissus* to safety despite her talkative and irresolute crew. Conrad's stories are concerned not only with the sea between men but also with the one between their words and acts.

While the young rebel talks of Conrad, the critic is planning how to mimic his voice when recounting the story; when the intruder talks of writing his own books, the critic stifles him with a comparison to Conrad; and when the younger man asks the older to write about him, the critic protests that he cannot write of what he fails to understand. Accused of self-interest, the burglar replies, "Man, your trouble is you don't listen hard enough" (172). Bereft of words, the young man expresses himself in the only way left: the *act*. By consigning the critic's words to the flames, he demonstrates their uselessness to him and, with his thumb cocked in a victory gesture, he expresses their worthlessness to his generation. Fowles's poem "Villagers" echoes the situation: "they want too much / I want too little / with my words."[5] Having planned his narrative as "a story to dine out on," the critic had wanted too little. But the intruder, wanting too much, has, by his act, gotten at least part of his wish: the critic *has* written his story. Not only has the encounter changed the critic in spite of his protest that he still misunderstands his junior, it has changed his writing as well. His reconstituted Peacock study will not be the same book he had begun; and his narrative, far above a tale "to dine out on," is a serious attempt to comprehend. It is humane, intelligent, and balanced, like Peacock's works. In showing improper father-son attitudes, as the title indicates, the younger and the older generations have been "poor clowns," but the narrator's story, itself a breakthrough, is more optimistic than its Old Cornish epigram. The ancient Cornish lost both land and language, but preservation of the word could save modern men from the same fate. Nonetheless, there is danger in today's linguistic polarization, as Fowles concludes in his poem "Protect the Word": "There seemed many great auks / Till the last one was killed."[6]

V *"The Enigma"*

Although "The Enigma" reveals the verbal poverty of the very wealthy British, with their indefinite pronoun-substitute "one," and the excessive rhetoric of the temporary liberal, the story has more to do with relating life's mystery to reality and fiction. Man has an instinct for solving mysteries, as the popularity of detective stories attests. But when a traditional detective story ends, the mystery ends with it; the fictional world is no pleasure anymore, until the reader begins a new book. Similarly, in reality, when man exposes mysteries—such as a woman's, for example—life is never quite the fun it had been. Having caught a mystery best left unsolved, man often lacks the restraint to throw it back, like the wrong fish. Fowles reveres mystery enough to have that restraint; and, with this story, he thrusts it upon his reader as well.

Although man has always followed mystery, today he often relies on professionals to do it for him. This story's professional, Detective Sergeant Michael Jennings, is given sole responsibility for tracing John Marcus Fielding only when no one in particular any longer wants him found. The family of the missing Member of Parliament are so emotionally crippled that they have trouble sustaining their feelings for him or for anyone else, for that matter. Some of his colleagues think he has absconded with a "dolly-bird," and the police, lacking a corpse, are busier elsewhere. But Michael, though he is their delaying tactic, has his duty as a professional solver of mysteries—until he meets one who is far better in the flesh than in solution.

Isobel Dodgson, the girl friend of the missing man's son, proves to be the sergeant's only good lead, and quite his prettiest. Isobel is also, as he tells her, the only character left in the story who is still *alive*, since she is free of upper-class pretense. In eventually choosing to leave her mystery unsolved, Michael chooses to preserve life itself, instead of siding with the sort of existential nonexistence promised by the likes of the surviving Fieldings. But his decision grows out of feeling for Isobel, for the living reality—not out of any theory, either existentialist or investigative. By admitting that Fielding had known her plan to be at the British Museum reading room, to which he has last been traced, Isobel links herself to the M.P.'s disappearance. But to Michael, her connection with events of the dead past becomes less important than her own living, and most alluring, reality.

As in each story in *The Ebony Tower*, Fowles relates life to art. Having already published a book of children's stories, Isobel is now writing a novel. Her novelist's view, while providing clues, also deepens the enigma. In telling Michael her private and "very literary" theory, she invites him to assume that "Nothing is real. All is fiction," that "somewhere there's someone writing us" (236). Having already suggested that Fielding had been dissatisfied with his life, she first obliquely describes one possible ending to their "detective story" in which she herself might have helped Fielding escape. Certain that such an ending cannot be proved, she carefully equates evidence with suspicion, pitying the writer, who has failed to plant leads and whose main character has walked out. Then, since there is no evidence in the story for her first hypothetical ending, she goes on to a "better" one. Having suggested that a system had "written" Fielding until he was just a fictional character, she points to his obsession with assuring himself that he is *known*. Her next ending for the story is the theory that Fielding, fossilized by circumstances (as Charles of *The French Lieutenant's Woman* might have been), decides to exit leaving his disappearance an enigma: "The one thing people never forget is the unsolved. Nothing lasts like a mystery" (242). She is suggesting that Fielding may have planned his own untraceable suicide to gain eternal repute in the manner of "God's trick": "Theologians talk about the *Deus absconditus*—the God who went missing? Without explaining why. That's why we've never forgotten him" (242). But one bit of evidence does not fit this second "fictional" ending: Michael observes, in parting, that it ignores Isobel's two unexplained hours after work that day. Having passed her "bird-brained fantasy" off as a joke, she mentions another novel she is considering, "a murder story": "Just the germ of an idea. When I can find someone to help me over the technical details" (246). They tacitly agree that Michael will be that someone, and Fowles ends the story with the two of them in bed—and John Marcus Fielding's disappearance, be it escape, suicide, or murder, still a mystery.

Michael, having halfheartedly and unsuccessfully applied to drag the pond suggested by Isobel's suicide theory, is not "inclined to blame John Marcus Fielding for anything at all" (247). If the M.P. has absconded, his absence has left Michael quite a mystery, the living part of which is Isobel. Fowles ended *The Magus* with a similar absconding which emphasized a related theological result: the creator's conferring absolute freedom through his nonpresence. If Fielding has indeed absconded, he has created his own mystery story, and since Isobel and Michael are now part of it, it is no wonder that the sergeant does not blame the creator. That "murder story" of Isobel's, her two hours not accounted for, her earlier suggestion of the M.P.'s repression as a "political animal," and her own fear of being alone with him all suggest perhaps another solution. But for Michael, the case is dead, and Isobel is alive: "it was not so much that he accepted her theory, but that like everyone else, though for a different reason, he now saw it didn't really matter. The act was done; taking it to bits, discovering how it had been done in detail, was not the point. The point was a living face with brown eyes, half challenging and half teasing; not committing a crime against that" (245).

If not the only detective story to end without a solution, this is certainly one of the few. But, as Michael, an experienced mystery-solver knows, the conventional, fully explained ending makes the traditional detective story less true to life. By leaving this one unsolved, he is being more faithful to life in two senses: both to the living Isobel, and to the way life really turns out. " 'So all our writer could really do is find a convincing reason why this main character had forced him to commit the terrible literary crime of not sticking to the rules?' She said, 'Poor man' " (239). Isobel pities Fowles unduly; his reason is ready: "The tender pragmatisms of flesh have poetries no enigma, human or divine, can diminish or demean— indeed, it can only cause them, and then walk out" (247). A notorious respecter of the *Deus absconditus*, Fowles gladly assumes such a role himself. As author, he walks out—leaving those fleshly poetries, and a mystery unforgettable because unsolved.

VI   "The Cloud"

"The Cloud," which Fowles considers the best story in *The Ebony Tower*, has predictably puzzled reviewers who object to its abstruseness. Unquestionably its structure is the strangest of the collection. Its narrative point of view varies from a bird's-eye, treetop perspective, through the minds of several characters, and in and out of what appears to be a written account by the protagonist. The point of view, sometimes elusive, relies extensively upon the indefinite "one" and shifts between past and present tenses about fifteen times, depending on how one counts. The effect is a narrative which destroys the reader's distinction between what has happened, what is happening, and what continually happens; in this story they are all the same. Parallels between the children and the adult characters further intensify the sense of timelessness.

As the final "variation" in this collection, "The Cloud" carries out a major theme in this and others of Fowles's books: the conflict between the brutalizing masculine ego and the civilizing female intelligence. Among the victims of the male, rape-oriented mentality are landscape, language, literature, and females themselves. The two men in this story are Peter and Paul, whose names place them as apostles of the same movement. Paul, like his biblical namesake, is the bearded and faintly ascetic writer, who takes refuge in an oxlike demeanor and readings of "The Scholar Gipsy." Peter, the aggressive apostle, is a grasping, egocentric television producer who hopes somehow to "use" the quiet French landscape around Paul's hideaway, an old converted mill. The mill's new use, as Paul's family retreat, might even be seen as a symbol of Paul's flight from the practical. Peter, on the other hand, is a selfish little "prick" who seeks to turn a profit from nature, both pastoral and human.

Along on the picnic outing which frames the story are three women: Paul's mother-goddess wife Bel, Peter's plaything girlfriend Sally, and Catherine, Bel's recently widowed sister. Peter has brought along his quiet little boy Tom, who plays with the two daughters of Paul and Bel. The elder daughter, Candida, is a budding authoritarian who mirrors a side of her mother's character; the younger girl, Emma, shares the less complacent, more imaginative introversion of her Aunt Catherine. The narrative and dialogue hint that Catherine is still mourning the death (perhaps a suicide) of her late poet husband. The obvious wish of the others that she get her mourning over with strongly resembles the situation in *Hamlet*, from which the story gets its epigram, as well as several explicit allusions.

Also like Hamlet, Catherine "does by thinking of doing" (299), although her role is often similar to Ophelia's—especially as she wanders away alone to the echo of Eliot's "Goonight. Goonight"— lines from "The Waste Land" which blend with Ophelia's "Goodnight, sweet ladies" and link modern absurdity to that of Elsinore. Looking on Paul as "dear ox," Catherine reflects that to manipulate him would be "to kill so capital a calf," then retreats to the speech of "a green girl" (271). Her sister Bel regrets that the story must be all *Hamlet*, "That wretched intellectual sob story, all walls and winds and winter puns. Willful flights from all simplicity. Absurd, to cast oneself as Hamlet; Ophelia perhaps, that one couldn't help at times. But the other needed such a perverse will, a deliberate choice" (295). Bel, placid Juno figure, cannot understand Catherine's refusal to be calm. Yet she, Catherine, Sally, and even little Emma, are wearing their rue with special differences.

The conflict in this story is as much verbal as sexual. Peter, the television-oriented snatcher of angles, having successfully bought both Paul and his landscape for canning into a special program, then tries to buy Catherine and her words—her translation of Roland Barthes's *Mythologies*. Especially important to the confrontation between Peter and Catherine are Barthes's views on what the media have done to undermine the reliability of language as a means of communication. Finally dismissing "bird-watching" and "word-watching" together, Peter tries a ploy to reduce the language issue to a television "angle"—rather, though the narrative does not say so, like Claudius asking to play in "The Mousetrap." Word-watching is at the root of this story; Peter, with his meaningless clichés— "incredible," "fantastic," "but I mean, you know," "Good God"— represents the mentality which has deprived language of its meaning. Bird-watching, too, is at the story's root, for the likes of Peter are ruining nature, as well. Much of the narrative, from within the "blessed sanctuary" of the indefinite "one," is from the viewpoint of what birds might see of human creatures: "if one had been a watching bird in the leaves, one would have seen them disappear . . ." (312). The owl's "woo-a-whit-too" and the oriole's searching cry of "Florio" provide the story a mythic timelessness.

In embracing the deathly, serpentine role of seductress, Catherine lures Peter from his "goat-track" into a sexual encounter with death. Their mutually hostile coupling is a sort of murder-suicide in which Catherine, in submitting, symbolically kills them both. Then, like the princess in her story, she is left alone in the wilderness—but with the added omen of a formidable storm cloud. The huge black cloud, nature's representation of the Ebony Tower, figuratively threatens not only Catherine but the entire party as well—especially sensitive little Emma, who may wear her rue as Catherine does, and Sally, who wears hers differently as Peter's sex doll. Like the deathlike Ebony Tower, and like the lowering thunderheads in Henry Breasley's *Kermesse*, the dark cloud menaces all that is wordless, inhuman, and frozen like Catherine in the relentless present tense.

CHAPTER 6

Lasting Fiction

I *Dorset's New Naturalist*

JOHN Fowles has established himself as one of today's few novelists whose reputation will outlast the century. His naturalism is as vivid as Hardy's, and his powerful sense of place joins his fiction to English literature's landscape-conscious tradition that dates back to the *Beowulf* and *Pearl* poets. Because this master storyteller uses old narrative tricks along with his own new ones, reading his books is usually an exciting experience. But his fiction's depth is the quality which helps it wear so well; its themes are timeless and universal yet important to twentieth century culture. Fowles does not simply *describe* humanity's contemporary dilemma; he gives his protagonists intelligence and strength of will to adapt positively along with a universe whose main premise is evolution in a system governed by both chance and natural law. He has such faith in human feeling and will that he shows these natural powers occasionally triumphing over deterministic forces. Fowles's enlightened positiveness—almost as cautious as Housman's—is the virtue which distinguishes his naturalism from Hardy's. The old Dorset naturalist chafed at hazard; the new one celebrates it.

II The French Lieutenant's Woman

Fowles's third novel, *The French Lieutenant's Woman*, stands among his finer efforts. Although the book's success depends largely upon chatty Victorian narrative, its plot proceeds with wit so lively, suspense so pleasant, and observations so intelligent that the novel instructs the reader without failing to delight him. Through this entertaining book, Fowles shows how man's existential awareness has helped him adapt to the loneliness of modern existence. And, while relating novel-writing to theology and social change to biol-

131

ogy, Fowles makes his reader care about Charles and Sarah despite
his ironic tone.

The French Lieutenant's Woman is structured like a traditionally
well-made novel, but with variations. The book's principal ex-
perimentation is with narrative viewpoint—a special blend of
modern and Victorian which is neither quite Victorian nor quite
modern. With old techniques carrying new messages, the novel is a
tribute to the Victorian tradition and a credit to the modern one. Its
narrator once hints that he may be trying to "pass off" a book of
essays on us: he is doing more than that, but he *does* give us the
essays, which we modern readers do not mind accepting from his
Victorian persona. From behind that old mask, Fowles presents
such themes as existential evolution more directly than contemporary techniques permit, finally showing that existential awareness
confronted people long before the French named it in the 1940s.
His Sarah Woodruff and Charles Smithson become as plausibly
conscious of their isolation in the nineteenth century as do heroes of
Sartre and Camus.

III   The Collector

The Collector has stood time's test, and the first novel Fowles
published remains one of his better works. This neat and simply
designed book which enjoyed such popular success has kept its
reputation among critics as well. *The Collector* has a structure so
concise and potent that the book qualifies as a little masterpiece.
Aside from flashbacks recalled by the two first-person narrators, the
plot is essentially that of a well-made novel, its primarily
chronological structure effectively maintaining suspense.

As a literary document, *The Collector* marks the end of British
fiction's preoccupation with picaresque, lower-class antiheroes. Its
villain is lower-class and his victim middle-class—a reversal which
breaks the tradition behind Britain's previous two decades of
social-conscious fiction sympathetic to the angry rebel. Justly
enough, Fowles shows how the establishment's inequity has conditioned Clegg's evil, but sympathy for the villain does not obscure
his crime's horror.

IV   The Magus

The strangeness of *The Magus* has provoked mixed critical reaction, but many of the novel's detractors strain too much at *classifying* it. In truth, the book only remotely resembles other works in contemporary English. Its shade is sometimes nearly Gothic, but its tone is closer kin to the old spirit of the Celtic French romance—and closer still to that of *Le Grand Meaulnes,* the book's more immediate French forebear. *The Magus* is also a relative of Richard Jefferies's *Bevis*—and even a remote cousin of Dickens's *Great Expectations.* These plots all send callow-but-bright heroes on quests fraught with mystery and sexual longing; as stories of adolescent initiation, these books are distinguished by their candid portrayals of sexuality and by their heroes' naive imaginations.

The revision of *The Magus* is generally an improvement over the original, although the book's first ending is more powerful and provocative than the simplified conclusion of the revision. Essentially the two versions of the novel are not different enough to be separate books, and I still consider the original one better than even Fowles thought it was. If the novel falls short of his intentions, it does so because of its grand design. Although Fowles connects its themes impressively, he has put more into the structure of both versions than novelists usually ask a plot to carry. As some critics have suggested, perhaps the book is too long, with too complex a plot, too many themes, and too many motifs. But because the novel is Fowles's first, and so intensely personal, one may forgive the young writer for attempting so much. The marvel is that he succeeded—whatever the book's flaws. *The Magus* accomplishes a revolutionary feat by rescuing the modern hero from hopelessness and restoring to him the possibility of love. Few modern novelists give their heroes such enlightenment or such freedom to exercise will based upon feeling.

V   The Ebony Tower

The title story of *The Ebony Tower* is as neat and compact a work as *The Collector.* Both stories concern the sometimes extreme shifts which upset equilibrium between countersupporting forces—in both society and art. But the shorter work focuses particularly upon certain problems that accompany imbalances in human feeling. It shows conflicts in history's continuing struggle between the fire of romantic excess and the frigidity of pure reason—in art and politics as well as in sexuality and love. "The Ebony Tower" employs the same medieval quest motif which charac-

terizes *The Magus,* and the shorter story is a variation on several
of that earlier book's themes. Fowles takes particular care to tie
the modern story to the ancient form by following it in the book
with his translation of the Celtic romance *Eliduc.* By so doing, he
strengthens the reader's sense that centuries of human behavior
have not invalidated the age-old quest which man still pursues—
despite its contradictions.

"Poor Koko," the next story in the collection, has little of the
knightly quest motif, because its narrator is a wielder of words—to
the exclusion of action. The simple story is a ruminative but
fast-moving recollection of a strange encounter between society's
verbal opposites: the youth deprived of skill in using his own
language and the older man complacently misusing his word power.
The brief story fairly portrays each side with such sensitivity that it
even suggests a constructive approach to solving the social problem.

"The Enigma" reveals another facet of the quest motif, following
the detective-story technique which began with Poe and gained
popularity with the work of Conan Doyle. But Fowles has done
something revolutionary, if we measure "The Enigma" against other
stories in its genre. Detective stories follow the motif of *solving*
mysteries, but Fowles presents the mystery, with all of its available
evidence, then blatantly leaves the enigma intact. Such an unusual
outcome is not caprice on his part; he shows that the important
mystery is life—far more precious than an unexplained death. His
hero-detective opts for life when he abandons his quest—tacitly
admitting that his living suspect is more considerable than a missing
Conservative Member of Parliament who, even if surviving, represents an upper class more dead than alive. The story is one of the
better examples of Fowles's skill, and we come away from it with a
powerful sense that life *is* mystery—and that explaining it away
would be more destructive than accepting the unknowable—or at
least the unknown.

"The Cloud," last in the collection, is a strange piece about which
critics have generally avoided comment. Its constantly shifting
tenses make the story difficult to read, but Fowles seems to be
moving the story's viewpoint toward a special timelessness—a sense
that certain acts are past, while others remain always in the present.
The narrative point of view in "The Cloud" becomes further compli-
cated when we realize that we are apparently seeing the action
through the eyes of birds. Such a viewpoint rather implies a
uniquely ironic objectivity: bird-as-people-watcher. "The Cloud"

draws the collection to its conclusion with a special thread of unity. The image of the tower of ebony functions, after all, as a metaphor for that darkly frightening sacrifice of human feeling which has accompanied this century's reaction against romantic extremes. Virtually every story in the collection centers upon the same theme: modern man's sometimes excessive control over his own feelings— the opposite of the problem facing his medieval ancestors. The ominous cloud overshadowing the book's end portends the deathly aftermath of man's male-female relationships deteriorating into emotionless, mutual exploitation. This durable thread of unity connects the book's parts in much the same way common themes unify Joyce's *The Dubliners*. By this book, as by his others, Fowles shows himself an astute scientist of human behavior—especially actions and thoughts viewed in their historical context. Through his fiction, he dramatizes the history of mankind's ideas by demonstrating how people behave.

VI   Daniel Martin

Daniel Martin is a lovely, profound novel which only remotely resembles Fowles's earlier fiction. Readers have responded to the book generally less enthusiastically than they greeted his more flamboyant works. Undeniably, *Daniel Martin* reads slower than the fiction in which Fowles often makes his narrative personae tease the reader and hold him in suspense. But even though something of a wizard at wielding an array of narrative techniques, Fowles has never seemed to feel quite right about doing it. Before *Daniel Martin*, he often acknowledged that the novelist's role was something less than honest—that crafting an appealing novel requires the writer to hide behind various masks while manipulating the reader with a series of ruses. In the foreword to his single volume of poems, Fowles embraced poetry as the more candid, less artificial art and only half jokingly called the novel "first cousin to a lie."

At last, after seven years in the writing, *Daniel Martin* is Fowles's attempt to create a novel devoid of all artifice. The book contains no monumental surprises, no close calls except for a remote Nazi bomber, and hardly any suspense. In fact, Fowles but lightly develops Jane, the character he considers the novel's center. The less important Jenny appears more real most of the time than does Jane, although Fowles identifies Jane, the object of Daniel's autumnal romantic quest, as *real*, Jenny as *ideal*. Jane's sometimes inanimate impression upon the reader is perhaps another result of Fowles's resolve to discard the artificial for the natural. He refuses to reach very far in revealing her character, keeping her as understated as her undemonstrative Englishness. Fowles may have sacrificed so much artifice in presenting Jane's character that she appeals only distantly to some readers. Nonetheless, by keeping her from the reader, he has succeeded in making her seem closer to Daniel, who seems, by his narrative reserve in describing her, to be holding her nearer his own heart.

Daniel Martin is positive and optimistic; several of its scenes are idyllically beautiful, others starkly impressive. Its power lies in its naturalism—its spontaneous style, restraint, and humanitarian wisdom. With this book, Fowles has succeeded in defending humanism as an institution and novel writing as a way of leaping the gaps that isolate people and centuries. He has created a book that reflects his own life—not only because of its autobiographical elements but also because of its kind and erudite character.

John Fowles has retained his kindness while bravely grappling with the most complex of mankind's dilemmas through his art. Fictionally demonstrating positive ways out of these dilemmas, Fowles has brought new hope to the stifled contemporary hero— and, by extension, to all of us. After earning a world-wide reputation for fiction full of tricks, he has had the temerity to abandon his tried techniques altogether for a frankly naturalistic novel—always promising mankind a solution. Although existentialism pervades Fowles's works, some of his simpler lines remain the more important—spoken by simple people like Dan's Aunt Millie, who reminds her nephew, "Hoping is no sin, Daniel." With his esteemed fiction, John Fowles has fired a new optimism in modern literary history, setting an example for today's writers with his genius, his courage, his humanity.

Notes and References

Chapter One

1. John Fowles, "Weeds, Bugs, Americans," *Sports Illustrated*, 33 (21 December 1970), 90, 95. Fowles disclaims responsibility for the "sickening" titles of this and his other essays published in popular American magazines.
2. Fowles, letter to Robert Huffaker, Lyme Regis, 12 September 1975; ellipses are Fowles's.
3. Fowles, "Weeds, Bugs, Americans," p. 86.
4. Fowles, letter to Huffaker, Lyme Regis, 3 July 1977; Alan W. Watts, *The Way of Zen* (New York: New American Library, 1957).
5. Fowles, Introduction to Sabine Baring-Gould, *Mehalah: A Story of the Salt Marshes* (1880; reprint ed., London: Chatto & Windus, 1969), p. vii.
6. *Poems* (New York: Ecco Press, 1973). I will not repeat this citation when my text refers to Fowles's other poems, since they are all from his only poetry volume.
7. Fowles, letter to Huffaker, Lyme Regis, 2 April 1974.
8. Fowles, in *World Authors 1950–1970*, ed. Wakeman, John (New York: H. W. Wilson, 1975), pp. 485–87.
9. Fowles, letter to Huffaker, Lyme Regis, 16 August 1978.
10. Charles Monaghan, "Portrait of a Man Reading," *Book World, Chicago Tribune* and *Washington Post*, 4 January 1970, p. 1.
11. Fowles, letter to Huffaker, 2 April 1974.
12. Fowles, *The Ebony Tower* (Boston: Little, Brown, 1974), p. 118.
13. Fowles, Epilogue to Claire de Durfort, *Ourika*, trans. John Fowles (Austin: W. Thomas Taylor, 1977), p. 56; *Ourika* was first published in 1824.
14. Fowles, letter to Huffaker, Lyme Regis, 18 April 1974. Henri Alain-Fournier, *Le Grand Meaulnes* (Paris: Editions Emile-Paul, 1913). The novel's first English translation, *The Wanderer*, trans. Françoise Delisle (Boston: Houghton Mifflin, 1928), has been reprinted: (New York: Doubleday, Anchor, 1953) and (Clifton, N.J.: Augustus M. Kelley, 1973). Fowles has written the afterword to the new translation, *The Wanderer*, trans. Lowell Bair (New York: Signet, 1971).
15. Ibid. (ellipses are Fowles's). For information about Alain-Fournier's life, I am indebted to Robert Gibson, *The Quest of Alain-Fournier* (New Haven: Yale University Press, 1954).
16. Fowles, letter to Huffaker, Lyme Regis, 16 August 1978.

17. Fowles, Foreword to *The Magus* (1965; rev. ed., Boston: Little, Brown, 1977), p. 8.

18. Ibid.

19. Ibid. pp. 8–9. Quotation immediately following this excerpt is from Fowles's comments in *Poems*, p. 2.

20. Fowles, Foreword to *The Magus*, rev. ed., p. 9.

21. Fowles, letter to Huffaker, Lyme Regis, 25 August 1978.

22. Ibid.

23. Fowles, letter to Huffaker, Lyme Regis, 3 July 1977.

24. Fowles, "Notes on an Unfinished Novel," in *Afterwards: Novelists on Their Novels*, ed. Thomas McCormack (New York: Harper & Row, 1969), p. 175.

25. Fowles, "On Being English But Not British," *The Texas Quarterly*, 7 (Autumn 1964), 154–62.

26. Daniel Halpern, "A Sort of Exile in Lyme Regis," *London Magazine*, 10 (March 1971), 34–46.

27. Fowles, "Hardy and the Hag," in *Thomas Hardy after Fifty Years*, ed. Lance St. John Butler (London: MacMillan, 1977). Fowles, who hints elsewhere at the oedipal drive in writing fiction, also mentions a similar kinship to Nabokov.

28. John Fowles, "Notes on Writing a Novel," *Harper's Magazine*, 237 (July 1968), 94. There were two early speculations about "the source" of *The French Lieutenant's Woman:* A. A. DeVitis and William J. Palmer, "*A Pair of Blue Eyes* Flash at *The French Lieutenant's Woman*," *Contemporary Literature*, 15 (Winter 1974), 90–101; and Phyllis Grosskurth, "*The French Lieutenant's Woman*," *Victorian Studies*, 16 (September 1972), 130–31. The latter suggests, on scant evidence, that Fowles may be "playing an elaborate joke on us" by having modeled his book on James Anthony Froude's little-known 1847 novella "The Lieutenant's Daughter." There are no parallels beyond the name and Froude's suggestion of a double ending; Fowles had never even heard of the book (letter, 2 April 1974). DeVitis and Palmer make valid points in suggesting the Hardy influence but are too eager to fix a single source. Fowles had, of course, read the Hardy novel, but its striking parallel to his own fossil imagery surprised him. "I have a memory for books of a totally non-academic kind. I cannot recall them consciously, often within a few weeks of reading them; but I recognize that they do get stored haphazardly somewhere lower down. The famous Soviet psychologist Luria once told me this is typical of many famous novelists . . . though I must confess I've never met one with quite my unique ability *not* to recall plot, names and the rest" (letter, 2 April 1974). Palmer's later study, *The Fiction of John Fowles* (Columbia: University of Missouri Press, 1974), advances Hardy and Dickens as the major influences upon *The French Lieutenant's Woman*. Fowles, who admires Dickens for creating his own world, acknowledges the impact of *Great Expectations*

upon *The Magus*, but I fail to see much Dickens in his third novel. Hardy's influence is unmistakable, though less specific and less a conscious phenomenon than it appears in Palmer's thesis.

29. Monaghan, p. 1.

30. Fowles, "Notes," p. 172.

31. Fowles, letter to Huffaker, Lyme Regis, 25 August 1978.

32. Fowles, letter to Huffaker, Lyme Regis, 18 April 1974; Richard Jefferies, *Bevis: The Story of a Boy* (1882; reprint ed., London: Eyre and Spottiswoode, 1948).

33. Fowles, letter to Huffaker, Lyme Regis, 16 July 1977.

34. Fowles, letter to Huffaker, Lyme Regis, 16 August 1978.

35. Fowles, letter to Huffaker, Lyme Regis, 5 October 1974.

36. Fowles, "Notes," p. 169.

37. Fowles, "The Trouble with Starlets," *Holiday*, 39 (June 1966), 12–20.

38. Fowles, *Daniel Martin* (Boston: Little, Brown, 1977), p. 402. Further page references to this edition appear parenthetically.

39. John Clare, *Selected Poems of John Clare*, ed. James Reeves (London: Heinemann, 1954).

40. Fowles, letter to Huffaker, Lyme Regis, 7 July 1978.

Chapter Two

1. John Fowles, letter to Robert Huffaker, Lyme Regis, 18 April 1974.

2. Fowles, letter to Huffaker, Lyme Regis, 12 September 1975. Fowles has commented in "Why I Rewrote *The Magus*," *Saturday Review* 18 February 1978 pp. 25–30, reprinted from the *London Times*. He further discusses his rewriting in his foreword to the revised edition.

3. "No Wise," *TLS*, 5 May 1966, p. 381.

4. Angus Wilson, "Fowles' Foul Fantasy," *Critic*, 25 (August 1966), 50–51, reprinted from *The Observer*, 1 May 1966, p. 27, under the equally sarcastic title "Making with the Metaphysics." Wilson was wrong about the film, too.

5. Anthony Burgess, in *The Listener*, 5 May 1966, p. 659; Burgess has since commented favorably on Fowles's work, especially in his understanding review of *Daniel Martin* [*The Irish Press*, 13 October 1977]. Despite Fowles's antipathy to reviewing others' fiction, he followed Burgess in 1978 for a year as monthly reviewer of contemporary Irish novels and short stories in *The Irish Press*.

6. Bill Byrom, in *The Spectator*, 6 May 1966, p. 574.

7. James R. Lindroth, in *America*, 114 (12 February 1966), 234.

8. Joseph Epstein, "An English Nabokov," *The New Republic*, 154 (19 February 1966), 26–29.

9. See also Ian Watt, in *The New York Times Book Review*, 9 November 1969, p. 1. Fowles comments further in an interview by James Campbell, in

Contemporary Literature, 17 (Autumn 1976), 455–69. Fowles's narrator firmly disallows mysticism, occultism, and drug cultures in *Daniel Martin* (Boston: Little, Brown, 1977).

10. Fowles, *The Aristos*, rev. ed. (Boston: Little, Brown, 1970), p. 49. Further references are parenthetic, preceded by "*A*," to distinguish them from pages in *The Magus*.

11. Fowles, *The Magus* (Boston: Little, Brown, 1965), p. 5, further references are parenthetic.

12. Fowles, *Daniel Martin*, p. 510.

13. Robert Scholes, "The Orgastic Fiction of John Fowles," *The Hollins Critic*, 6 (December 1969), 1–12.

14. See also Fowles's "I Write Therefore I Am," *Evergreen Review*, 8 (August–September 1964), 16–17, 89–90. Fowles titles his essay with Nick's Cartesian variant but makes clear his own affirming life rather than rejecting it. Nick tries to exist by expressing his rejection of banal reality. Fowles exists by being a writer involved with life.

15. Scholes, p. 7.

16. Ibid., pp. 1–3.

17. Thomas Stearns Eliot, *Four Quartets* (New York: Harcourt, Brace, 1943).

18. Homeopathic ritual imitates the event it seeks to bring about. See Sir James George Frazer, *The Golden Bough*, 1 vol. abridged ed. (New York: Macmillan, 1922).

19. John Fowles, letter to Robert Huffaker, Lyme Regis, 2 April 1974. My summary, from throughout Jung's works, is geared only to his theories most applicable to *The Magus*.

20. Carl G. Jung, *Collected Papers on Analytical Psychology* (London: Bailliere, Tindall and Cox, 1922), p. 468.

21. Carl G. Jung, *Contributions to Analytical Psychology* (London: Kegan Paul, Trench, Trubner, 1928), p. 35.

22. Ibid., p. 38.

23. Conchis's name echoes that of the conch shells, trumpets for the heralds of Poseidon, whose statue stands at Bourani's center: "perfect majesty because perfect control, perfect health, perfect adjustment" (482). Fowles writes, "As I've often said, only the sea-shell 'pun' was intended. Conchis/conscious offends me" (Letter to Huffaker, Lyme Regis, 8 April 1979).

24. Jung, *Contributions*, pp. 266–67.

25. Jung, *Collected Papers*, p. 238.

26. Ibid., p. 249.

27. Jung, *Contributions*, p. 57.

28. Marvin Magalaner, "The Fool's Journey: John Fowles's *The Magus*," in *Old Lines, New Forces*, ed. Robert K. Morris (Cranbury, N.J.: Associated University Presses, 1976). See also Arthur Edward Waite, *The Pictorial Key to the Tarot* (1910; reprint ed., New Hyde Park, New York:

University Books, 1959). A critical stretching links Alison's air-hostess job to the Tarot *air* (Delma E. Presley, "The Quest of the Bourgeois Hero," *Journal of Popular Culture*, 6 [Fall 1972], 394–98).

29. George E. Mylonas, *Eleusis and the Eleusinian Mysteries* (Princeton: Princeton University Press, 1961). Since human ritual is universal, ample religious parallels extend from the Orphic and Dionysian to the modern Christian. Cabalistic correspondences exist in everything from Rosicrucianism to the Order of the Golden Dawn. The Tarot Magus is linked to Apollo and to the Rosicrucian Magus. "Tarot" transliterates to Latin *Rota* ("wheel") and reads both ways on the Wheel card, being linked with Egyptian *Taro* ("royal way"), *Thoth* ("doctrine of mercury"), and the final syllables of Phonecian-Syrian Ash*toroth*, whose Egyptian name is Isis—and to whose Greek counterpart Astarte Fowles dedicates the book. Such parallels, however, merely support Jung's theory of universal archetypes; no mysticism underlies the novel.

30. Jung, in D. T. Suzuki, *Introduction to Zen Buddhism* (1934; reprint ed., New York: Philosophical Library, 1949). Jung further discusses alchemical and cabalistic parallels in *Alchemical Studies*, vol. 13 of *The Collected Works of Carl G. Jung*, ed. Herbert Read et al., 4th ed. (New York: Pantheon, 1967); *Mysterium Coniunctionis*, vol. 14 (1963); *Psychology and Alchemy*, vol. 12 (1953).

31. Fowles, letter to Huffaker, Lyme Regis, 12 September 1975.

32. Cf. Latin *muto, -onis* = "penis."

33. Jung, *Contributions*, pp. 127–28, 130, 200–201. Jung discusses the anima and animus elsewhere, but these citations most clearly indicate the concepts as they apply to Fowles's works.

34. Jung, *Collected Papers*, p. 457.

35. Jojo's clownishness echoes the sadly awkward Pierrot in *Le Grand Meaulnes*, and Alain-Fournier's linking the image to his "pretty Pierrot" Valentine, Alison's counterpart as the real, common, woman. Alain-Fournier, *Le Grand Meaulnes* (Paris: Editions Emile-Paul, 1913).

36. Eliot, *Four Quartets*.

37. Ezra Pound, *The Fifth Decad of Cantos* (Norfolk, Conn.: New Directions, 1937).

38. Alfred, Lord Tennyson, "The Beggar Maid," in *The Poetical Works of Alfred Tennyson* (Chicago: G. W. Borland, 1882), p. 309.

Chapter Three

1. John Fowles, "On Being English but Not British," *The Texas Quarterly*, 7 (Autumn 1964), 154–62.

2. "Miranda Removed," *Times Literary Supplement*, 17 May 1963, p. 353.

3. Honor Tracy, "Love Under Chloroform," *The New Republic*, 3 August 1963, pp. 20–21.

    4. Fowles, *The Collector* (Boston: Little, Brown, 1963), pp. 143–44.
Subsequent references to pages in this edition are parenthetic in the text.
    5. Carl G. Jung, *Contributions to Analytical Psychology*, trans. H. G.
and Cary F. Baynes (New York: Harcourt, Brace, London: Kegan Paul,
Trench, Trubner, 1928), p. 200.
    6. Fowles, *The Aristos*, rev. ed. (Boston: Little, Brown, 1970), p. 10.
Subsequent references to pages in this edition are parenthetic in the text,
preceded with "*A*," to distinguish them from pages in *The Collector*.
    7. Fowles, letter to Robert Huffaker, Lyme Regis, 17 June 1974.
    8. John Fowles, "I Write Therefore I Am," *Evergreen Review*, 8
(August–September 1964), 16–17, 89–90.
    9. Ibid., pp. 90, 17 (cf. "Stardom," *Poems*, a far less objective view of
the situation).

Chapter Four

    1. John Fowles, "Notes on Writing a Novel," *Harper's Magazine*, 237
(July 1968), 88–97. The quay is the Cobb of Lyme Harbor, which Fowles
could see from Underhill Farm. He wrote the entire novel there, in the
wooden hut beside the seventeenth-century farmhouse. He writes, "The
Cobb is just visible from the bottom of the farm garden, a mile or so away (I
now think its distance physically had something to do with the genesis of the
novel, of its looking-backwardness)" (Letter to Huffaker, Lyme Regis, 8
April 1979).
    2. Fowles, introduction to Sabine Baring-Gould, *Mehalah: A Story of
the Salt Marshes* (1880; reprint ed., London: Chatto & Windus, 1969), p. xi.
    3. Fowles, introduction to Claire de Durfort, *Ourika*. 1824; trans. John
Fowles (Austin: W. Thomas Taylor, 1977).
    4. Fowles, "Notes," p. 90.
    5. Walter Allen is the only critic who ever tried to dismiss the book as
only a historical novel ("The Achievement of John Fowles," *Encounter*, 35
[August 1970], 64–67). Allen says Fowles is "merely taking advantage of
hindsight in his interpretation of character and scene as historical novelists
have always done." He ignores that Fowles borrows elements of the
century-old style and uses conspicuously modern metaphor to describe
antique situations. Allen rightly compares Fowles's thirteenth chapter to
the seventeenth of *Adam Bede*, where Eliot interpolates an essay on her
characterization technique much as Fowles does. But Allen disregards
Fowles's entering the novel as character, and he disposes of the multiple
endings with, "One remembers the two endings of *Great Expectations*."
One does, but one also recalls that Dickens wrote the second as substitute
for the first, not as companion to it. Nor does Allen clarify whether he thinks
Adam Bede and *Great Expectations* are historical novels.
    6. Fowles, "Notes," p. 88.
    7. Ibid., p. 90.

8. Fowles first mentions the musical parallel in Richard Boston, "John Fowles, Alone But Not Lonely," *New York Times Book Review*, 9 November 1969, pp. 2, 52–53. Serge Prokofieff's *Classical Symphony*, Opus 25 (1917), was what its composer called an effort to write a symphony as Haydn or Mozart might have, had they lived in his day. Critics have described it with terms which might also apply to Fowles's novel. Robert Perlongo (recording: Columbia MS 6545) calls its *Allegro* in sonata form a "charming spoof" of stately court music two centuries older; he describes its *Larghetto* in ternary form as "delightful mock-elegance," its *Gavotte* as "deliberately heavy-handed yet beautifully engaging," and its *Finale* as a "sprightly take-off on the classical way of 'wrapping up' a symphony." To be more specific, Prokofieff's harmony and many of his rhythms (especially in the second movement) are modern, while orchestration, themes, dynamic contrasts, and structure of movements are classical. Fowles's analogue from *The Ebony Tower* (Boston: Little, Brown, 1974), is on p. 18.

9. John Fowles, *The French Lieutenant's Woman* (Boston: Little, Brown, 1969), p. 75. Subsequent citations from this edition are parenthetic in the text.

10. William Makepeace Thackeray, *Vanity Fair* (1864; reprint ed., New York: Random House, 1950), p. 730.

11. A few critics attacked Fowles's device of pleading autonomy for his characters, particularly Christopher Ricks ("The Unignorable Real," *The New York Review of Books*, 12 February 1970, pp. 22–24). Elizabeth D. Rankin sums the issue in "Cryptic Coloration in *The French Lieutenant's Woman*," *The Journal of Narrative Technique*, 3 (September 1973), 193–207. She calls Fowles's denying omnipotence "cryptic coloration" rendering his fiction acceptable among contemporaries. I consider his demurrer stronger than such conformity, since it supports his positive theological views. Rankin's good sense lies in recognizing that Fowles's insistence upon his characters' freedom is a *device* rather than some effort to make the reader believe that they are really independent of him. Fowles elsewhere discusses the novelist's obligation to manage characters instead of letting them usurp control of the plot. He does not mean that his characters actually take over and dictate their own fictional behavior: "I suggest that characters *do* do that. But that's not really what I believe. For a time they're just wooden tailor's dummies with clothes on, and suddenly they start up on their own. . . . [Y]ou get this bizarre experience when you feel they know the lines they ought to be saying, and you're searching around in the dark to find out. . . . But of course in reality the writer has the final say" (Daniel Halpern and John Fowles, "A Sort of Exile in Lyme Regis," *London Magazine*, 10 [March 1971], 34–46).

12. Fowles, *The Aristos* (Boston: Little, Brown, 1964), pp. 22, 26. Further references to this edition are cited parenthetically, preceded by *A* to distinguish them from citations of the novel.

13. Bradford Booth, "Form and Technique in the Novel," *The Rein-*

terpretation of Victorian Literature, ed. Joseph E. Baker (Princeton: Princeton University Press, 1950), pp. 94–96. Booth has reportedly since modified this view.

14. Anthony Trollope, *Barchester Towers* (1857; reprint ed., New York: Rinehart, 1949), pp. 142–43. Numerous other critics, notably J. W. Beach, have singled out this passage for attack.

15. George Eliot, *Adam Bede* (1867; reprint ed., New York: Rinehart, 1948), p. 178. Walter Allen's article (n. 5, above) makes its best comparison to this chapter of Eliot's.

16. For the best discussion of open and closed endings, see Alan J. Friedman, *The Turn of the Novel* (New York: Oxford University Press, 1966).

17. Had Sarah's bleeding been caused by menstruation or "spotting," the likelihood of conception would have been almost zero, although such does not appear to be Fowles's intent. Any gynecology textbook will testify that damage to the hymen during a virgin's first intercourse may be accompanied by varying degrees of bleeding. An extreme flow of blood follows the rupture of an imperforate hymen, a relatively rare phenomenon.

18. Natural radiation in the form of gamma rays may affect fertilization in various ways, related to spermatogenesis, ovulation, sperm motility, and egg implantation. But the most significant link of the gamma ray to evolution, as described in the Gardner epigram, is its role in genetic mutation. As a factor in this particular evolutionary process, the gamma ray not only modifies the characteristics of living organisms but also might have inhibited Lalage's birth in either of two ways: first, by genetically affecting the fertility of either one parent or both, and second, by causing mutation of lethal genes, which may destroy life at any time, including the embryonic and the fetal stages. My judgment is founded in, among other sources, the following: Theodosius Grigorievich Dobzhansky, *Genetics of the Evolutionary Process* (New York: Columbia University Press, 1970); and Eldon John Gardner, *Principles of Genetics* (New York: John Wiley & Sons, 1968). Fowles again mentions the genetics of evolution in *Daniel Martin*, p. 526.

19. Carl G. Jung, *Contributions to Analytical Psychology*, trans. H. G. and Cary F. Baynes (New York: Harcourt, Brace, 1928), p. 170.

20. The very etymology of the originally medical term "hysteria" is a nice bit of male sexism: the word developed from Greek *hyster* ("uterus") and initially denoted a peculiarly feminine affliction.

21. Jung, *Contributions*, p. 168.

22. Ibid., p. 174.

23. Ibid., pp. 171–72.

24. Ibid., p. 169.

25. Fowles's closing with Sarah's likeness to the Sphinx is fitting in another context, because "The Sphinx," or "The Question," was among Rosetti's unfinished paintings. In 1875, he had drawn the motif in pencil— showing man's three phases (Youth, Maturity, and Age) confronting the

riddle of a bare-breasted Sphinx who resembles his model Jane Morris.
Jane, I like to think, resembles Sarah, although Fowles says that he
envisioned Sarah as more like Rosetti's late wife, Elizabeth Siddal, the
painter's other principal model.

Chapter Five

1. John Fowles, *The Ebony Tower* (Boston: Little, Brown, 1974), p. 41.
Subsequent citations from this edition's stories are included parenthetically
in the text.

2. I draw my conclusions on the Italian quattrocento, in part, from
these sources: Edith R. Abbot, *The Great Painters* (New York: Harcourt,
Brace, 1927); Edward Armstrong, *History and Art in the Quattrocento*
(London: Oxford University Press, 1923); Oscar Hagen, *Art Epochs and
Their Leaders* (New York: Scribner's, 1927); Frank J. Mather, Jr., *A History
of Italian Painting* (New York: Henry Holt, 1923); and E. G. Salter, *Nature
in Italian Art* (London: A. & C. Black, 1912).

3. Breasley's linking the vulva to the mouse is hardly a new idea, what
with centuries of puns on "mousehole" and bawdy references to the mouse
as a furry little thing to be pursued (cf. today's "beaver"). The weasel,
another little furry creature, is the mouse's notorious enemy, as well as
being the traditional animal symbol of the wicked and alluring young
woman, reputedly sleeping each night in a different lair. The weasel was
sometimes said to conceive through the ear and give birth through the
mouth, thus spreading deceptive reports of what she had heard, or, in some
Christian contexts, resembling the Virgin by conceiving and giving birth to
God's Son, the Word. To the ancient Egyptians, she symbolized speech.
Other legends report her to conceive orally and deliver aurally, her
punishment for, in the person of the witch Galanthis, having delayed the
birth of Hercules. Leviticus 11:29 classifies her unclean, and she has long
been identified with faithlessness. She had the traditional power to revive
her own kind with the proper herb. But with her decidedly bad reputation
as seductress, it is no wonder that Chaucer compares the lithe body of
Alisoun in "The Miller's Tale" to that of a weasel—probably the first such
reference in English literature. See E. Talbot Donaldson, *Speaking of
Chaucer* (New York: Norton, 1970), p. 22; and John Livingston Lowes,
Geoffrey Chaucer (Bloomington: Indiana University Press, 1958), p. 177.
The weasel's redeeming function was her traditional enmity to the serpent,
a near relative of the dragon. But she could only conquer the snake after
fortifying herself by partaking of rue, the bitter herb associated by pun with
regret. Many a seductress, of course, has taken such rue to defeat the
dragon, with its fiercely sexual symbolism. The weasels in both *Eliduc* and
"The Ebony Tower" are particularly linked to dragon lore, since the red
flower, symbolic of the dragon's blood, was said to have sprung from the
earth where St. George made his kill—having first used the mesmerized

beast to blackmail the city into accepting Christianity. See Angelo de Gubernatis, *Zoological Mythology or The Legends of Animals* (1872; reprint ed., Detroit: Singing Tree Press, 1968); Christina Hole, *Saints in Folklore* (New York: M. Barrows, 1965); Ernest Ingersoll, *Dragons and Dragon Lore* (New York: Payson & Clarke, 1928); Beryl Rowland, *Animals with Human Faces* (Knoxville: University of Tennessee Press, 1973); and T. H. White, *The Bestiary: A Book of Beasts* (New York: G. P. Putnam's Sons, 1954).

4. The weasel's English name is literally a bad one. It comes from the Anglo-Saxon *wesle*, which in turn stems from the probable Indo-European base *weis-*, to flow out. The latter stem refers to its pungent musk, comparable to the Latin *vis(s)io*, an unpleasant smell. Its Greek name, *mustela*, literally means "long mouse," further linking Diana and the weasel. Its French name, *belette*, is the only one of these with decent etymological connotations: its roots are the same as *belvédère* (from *belle vue*), literally, a pretty view; now, a small terrace with a view. See n. 3, above.

5. Fowles, *Poems* (New York: Ecco, 1973).

6. Ibid.

Selected Bibliography

PRIMARY SOURCES

1. Novels, Translations, and Other Books

The Aristos: A Self-Portrait in Ideas. Boston: Little, Brown, 1964, rev. ed.,
    1970; London: Jonathan Cape, 1965, rev. ed., 1968.
Cinderella, by Charles Perrault. 1697; translated by John Fowles. Boston:
    Little, Brown, 1976; London: Jonathan Cape, 1974.
The Collector. Boston: Little, Brown, 1963; London: Jonathan Cape, 1963.
Daniel Martin. Boston: Little, Brown, 1977; London: Jonathan Cape, 1977.
The Ebony Tower. Boston: Little, Brown, 1974; London: Jonathan Cape,
    1974.
The Enigma of Stonehenge. Summit Books, 1980 (tentative). London:
    Jonathan Cape, 1980.
The French Lieutenant's Woman. Boston: Little, Brown, 1969; London:
    Jonathan Cape, 1969.
Islands. Boston: Little, Brown, 1978; London: Jonathan Cape, 1978.
The Magus. Boston: Little, Brown, 1965, rev. ed., 1977; London: Jonathan
    Cape, 1965, rev. ed., 1977.
Ourika, by Claire de Durfort. 1824; translated by John Fowles. Austin: W.
    Thomas Taylor, 1977.
Poems. New York: Ecco Press, 1973; Toronto: Macmillan Co. of Canada
    Ltd., 1973.
Shipwreck. Boston: Little, Brown, 1975; London: Jonathan Cape, 1974.
Steep Holm—A Case History in the Study of Evolution. Coauthored with
    Rodney Legg. London: Kenneth Allsop Memorial Trust, 1978.
The Tree. Boston: Little, Brown, 1980; London: Aurum Press, 1979.

2. Essays, Forewords, etc.

Afterword to *The Wanderer (Le Grand Meaulnes),* by Henri Alain-
    Fournier. 1913; translated by Lowell Bair. New York: New American
    Library, 1971.
Foreword to *Hawker of Morwenstow: Portrait of a Victorian Eccentric,* by
    Piers Brendon. London: Jonathan Cape, 1975.
Foreword and Afterword to *The Hound of the Baskervilles,* by Sir Arthur
    Conan Doyle. 1902; reprint ed., London: John Murray and Jonathan
    Cape, 1974.

Foreword to *The Lais of Marie de France*, by Marie de France. Translated and introduced by Robert Hanning and Joan Ferrante. New York: E. P. Dutton, 1978.

"Hardy and the Hag." In *Thomas Hardy After Fifty Years*, edited by Lance St. John Butler, pp. 28–42. London: Macmillan, 1977.

Introduction, Glossary and Appendix to *Mehalah: A Story of the Salt Marshes*, by Sabine Baring-Gould. 1880; reprint ed., London: Chatto & Windus, 1969.

"Is the Novel Dead?" *Books*, 1 (Autumn 1970), 2–5.

"I Write Therefore I Am." *Evergreen Review*, 8 (August–September 1964), 16–17, 89–90.

"Jacqueline Kennedy Onassis and Other First (and Last) Ladies." *Cosmopolitan*, October 1970, pp. 144–49.

"*The Magus* Revisited." *London Times*, 28 May 1977, p. 7. Reprinted as "Why I Rewrote *The Magus*." *Saturday Review*, 18 February 1978, pp. 25–30. An expanded version of the revised edition's foreword.

"Making a Pitch for Cricket." *Sports Illustrated*, 21 May 1973, pp. 100–103.

"Marriage, Passion, Love: My Side of the Dialogue." *Vogue*, 15 November 1964, pp. 114–15. Excerpts from *The Aristos*.

"My Recollections of Kafka." *Mosaic*, 3 (Summer 1970), 31-41. Reprinted in *New Views of Franz Kafka*, edited by R. G. Collins and Kenneth McRobbie (Winnepeg, Canada: University of Manitoba Press, 1974).

"Notes on Writing a Novel." *Harper's Magazine*, 237 (July 1968), pp. 88–97. Reprinted as (1) "On Writing a Novel," *The Cornhill Magazine*, 1060 (Summer 1969), 281–95; (2) "Notes on an Unfinished Novel," in *Afterwards: Novelists on Their Novels*, edited by Thomas McCormack, pp. 160–75; (New York: Harper & Row, 1969); and (3) in *The Novel Today*, edited by Malcolm Bradbury, London: Fontana-Collins, 1977. The Thackeray example (*Cornhill*, pp. 287–88) is absent from *Harper's*, whose final paragraph is cut from the *Cornhill* version.

"On Being English but Not British." *The Texas Quarterly*, 7 (Autumn 1964), 154–62.

"Remembering Cruikshank." *Library Chronicle*, 35 (1973), xiii–xvi.

"Seeing Nature Whole." *Harper's Magazine*, 259 (November 1979), 49–68.

"The Trouble with Starlets." *Holiday*, June 1966, pp. 12–20.

"Weeds, Bugs, Americans." *Sports Illustrated*, 21 December 1970, pp. 84–88.

Untitled essay in *Bookmarks*, edited by Frederic Raphael, pp. 53–57 (London: Jonathan Cape, 1975). Reprinted as "Of Memoirs and Magpies," *Atlantic*, 235 (June 1975), 82–84.

3. Poems Published Individually

"Amor Vacui," "It is a Lie." *Antaeus*, 9 (Spring 1973), 68–69.

"By the Appian Way," "At Ostia." *Antaeus*, 1 (Summer 1970), 20–21.

"Crusoe," "Aboulia." *Mademoiselle*, May 1973, p. 160. These poems are identical texts to their printing in *Poems*, except for a period to the last line of "Aboulia" in *Mademoiselle*, none in *Poems*.

"In Paradise." *Transatlantic Review*, 14 (Autumn 1963), 9–15. A dramatic poem consisting of all dialogue, with intercalated headings taken almost verbatim from his own poem "A Village Between." That previously unpublished poem was later to appear in *TR*, 16 (Summer 1964), and in *Poems*, slightly revised and titled "At a Village Between."

"Mirage." *Antaeus*, 1 (Summer 1970), 22.

"A Village Between," "Unasked," "Villagers." *Transatlantic Review*, 16 (Summer 1964), 36–37. The first and last of these poems appear with minor changes in *Poems*. The Lines from "A Village Between" were first published as intercalated headings to the long dramatic poem "In Paradise" (*TR*, 14 [Autumn 1963], 9–15).

4. Book Reviews, Nonfiction

"All Too Human." *Birds, Beasts, and Men*, by H. R. Hays. *New Statesman*, 20 July 1973, pp. 90–91.

"Aperitifs." *Companion Guide to Devon and Cornwall*, by Darrell Bates. *New Statesman*, 11 June 1976, pp. 785–86.

"Bleeding Hearts." *The Akenham Burial Case*, by Ronald Fletcher. *New Statesman*, 14 June 1974, pp. 842–43.

"Come to Britain?" *Circles and Standing Stones*, by Evan Hadingham. *New Statesman*, 5 December 1975, pp. 728–29.

"Confined Species." *The Ark in the Park*, by Wilfred Blunt; *London's Zoo*, by Gwynne Vevers; *Golden Days*, by Lord Zuckerman. *New Statesman*, 7 May 1976, pp. 612–14.

"Country Matters." *Finches*, by Ian Newton; *The Pollination of Flowers*, by Michael Procter and Peter Yeo. *New Statesman*, 27 April 1973, pp. 620–21.

"Death on the Ocean Wave." *Supership*, by Noël Mostert; *Death Raft*, by Alexander McKee. *New Statesman*, 4 July 1975, pp. 22–24.

"For the Dark." *The Death of Narcissus*, by Morris Fraser. *New Statesman*, 18 February 1977, pp. 221–22.

From Cliche to Archetype, by Marshall McLuhan, with Wilfred Watson. *Saturday Review*, 21 November 1970, pp. 32–33.

"Gory Details." *Blood: The Paramount Humour*, by Earl Hackett. *New Statesman*, 9 March 1973, pp. 345–46.

"Guide to a Man-Made Planet." *The World of Charles Dickens*, by Angus Wilson. *Life*, 4 September 1970, pp. 8–9.

"Horse Magic." *The Days that We Have Seen*, by George Evart Evans. *New Statesman*, 1 August 1975, p. 148.

"Ivory Towers." *Lighthouse*, by Tony Parker. *New Statesman*, 9 May 1975, pp. 628–29.

"Late Harvest." *The Worm Forgives the Plough*, by John Stewart Collis. *New Statesman*, 26 October 1973, pp. 612–13.

"A Lost World." *Lark Rise to Candleford*, by Flora Thompson. *New Statesman*, 3 August 1973, pp. 154–55.

"Menhirs Maketh Man." *Beyond Stonehenge*, by Gerald S. Hawkins; *The Old Stones of Land's End*, by John Michell. *New Statesman*, 22 March 1974, pp. 412–13.

"Missing Beats." *Autobiography*, by Margiad Evans. *New Statesman*, 13 September 1974, p. 352.

"The Most Secretive of Victorian Writers, a Kind of Giant Mouse." *Thomas Hardy: Distance and Desire*, by J. Hillis Miller. *New York Times Book Review*, 21 June 1970, p. 4.

"Other Edens." *Landscapes and Seasons of the Medieval World*, by Derek Pearsall and Elizabeth Salter. *New Statesman*, 12 October 1973, pp. 524–25.

"Outlook Unsettled." *Times of Feast, Times of Famine*, by Emmanuel LeRoy Ladurie. *New Statesman*, 26 January 1973, pp. 130–31.

"The Rambler." *The Naturalist in Britain*, by David Elliston Allen. *New Statesman*, 6 August 1976, pp. 183–84.

"Royal Stews." *The Cleveland Street Scandal*, by H. Montgomery Hyde. *New Statesman*, 19 March 1976, pp. 362–64.

"Softer than Beef." *Alive*, by Piers Paul Read. *New Statesman*, 10 May 1974, pp. 664–65.

"A Study in Scarlet." *The Adventures of Conan Doyle*, by Charles Higham. *New Statesman*, 26 November 1976, pp. 751–52.

"Unnatural Habitats." *The Unofficial Countryside*, by Richard Mabey; *Insects of Britain and Northern Europe*, by Michael Chinery; *The Book of Flowers*, by Alice M. Coats. *New Statesman*, 14 December 1973, p. 912.

"Voices of the Deep." *Whales, Dolphins and Seals*, by D. E. Gaskin; *Man's Place*, by Karl-Erik Fichtelius and Sverre Sjolander. *New Statesman*, 15 June 1973, pp. 892–93.

5. Reviews of Irish Fiction, in *The Irish Press*, 1978, as Guest Reviewer for the Thursday "Book Page," Edited by David Marcus. (listed in order of publication)

"On Target." *Out of Focus*, by Alf MacLochlainn. 12 January.

"Downandoutdom." *Four Novellas*, by Samuel Beckett. 16 February.

"The Nature of Irishness." *Selected Stories of Sean O'Faolain*, by Sean O'Faolain. 13 April.

"Sidesteps." *The Destinies of Darcy Dancer, Gentleman*, by J. P. Donleavy. 1 June.

"Irish Keys." *Getting Through*, by John McGahern; *Mrs. Reinhardt and Other Stories*, by Edna O'Brien. 15 June.

"Central Values." *Lovers of Their Time*, by William Trevor. 28 September.
"Crime and Punishment." *Bogmail*, by Patrick McGinley. 19 October.
"Mainstream and Sidestream." *Paddy No More: Modern Irish Short Stories*, edited by William Vorm. 28 December.

SECONDARY SOURCES

1. Criticism and Bibliography

ALLEN, WALTER. "The Achievement of John Fowles." *Encounter*, 35 (August 1970), 64–67. Acknowledges Fowles as a brilliant storyteller but attempts to classify *The French Lieutenant's Woman* as merely a good historical novel whose experimental elements are "a boring red herring."

BERETS, RALPH. "*The Magus:* A Study in the Creation of a Personal Myth." *Twentieth Century Literature*, 19 (April 1973), 89–98. Discusses the hero's ordeal as an efficacious modern myth to stand against contemporary meaninglessness.

BINNS, RONALD. "John Fowles: Radical Romancer." *Critical Quarterly*, 15 (Winter, 1973), 317–34. Observes that Fowles merges a romantic theory of creativity with a realistic view of life. An enlightened discussion of Fowles's writings through *The French Lieutenant's Woman*.

BRADBURY, MALCOLM. "John Fowles's *The Magus*." In *Sense and Sensibility in Twentieth-Century Writing*, edited by Brom Weber, pp. 26–38. Carbondale: Southern Illinois University Press, 1970. Admiringly analyzes *The Magus* as a positive artistic gesture. A brilliant reading of the novel.

BRANTLINGER, PATRICK; ADAM, IAN; and ROTHBLATT, SHELDON. "*The French Lieutenant's Woman:* A Discussion." *Victorian Studies*, 15 (March 1972), 339–56. Focuses upon the novel's thematic and historical significance. Valuable primarily for Adam's and Rothblatt's views.

CHURCHILL, THOMAS. "Waterhouse, Storey, and Fowles: Which Way Out of the Room?" *Critique*, 10 (Summer 1968), 72–87. Cleverly assesses the positive impact of *The Collector* and *The Magus* upon the contemporary hero's imprisoned state: Fowles has either beaten the "room" or else "varied the enclosure."

CORBETT, THOMAS. "The Film and the Book: A Case Study of *The Collector*." *English Journal*, 57 (March 1968), 328–33. Considers how well the film reflects the book's central metaphors.

COSTA, RICHARD HAUER. "Trickery's Mixed Bag: The Perils of Fowles' *French Lieutenant's Woman*." *Rocky Mountain Review of Language and Literature*, 29, no. 1 (1975), 1–9. Contrasts Fowles's showing versus his telling, characterizing the novel's triumph as the narrative and didactic rather than the dramatic. Against Walter Allen's view, considers the novel as both historical and experimental.

DETWEILER, ROBERT. "The Unity of John Fowles' Fiction." *Notes on Contemporary Literature*, 1 (March 1971), 3–4. Simply notes the common theme of *possession* in Fowles's first three novels.

DEVITIS, A. A., and PALMER, WILLIAM J. "*A Pair of Blue Eyes* Flash at *The French Lieutenant's Woman*." *Contemporary Literature*, 15 (Winter 1974), 90–101. Too eagerly tries to confine Fowles's "source" to the single Hardy novel, while astutely illuminating a striking parallel in fossil imagery. Misinterprets the hero's isolation in the final, existentialist, ending.

DIXON, TERRELL F. "Expostulation and a Reply: The Character of Clegg in Fowles and Sillitoe." *Notes on Contemporary Literature*, 4, no. 2 (1974), 7–9. Notes Sillitoe's Clegg (*A Start in Life*, 1970) as a reply to Fowles's Clegg (*The Collector*, 1963). Fowles's heroine attacks Sillitoe's earlier novel *Saturday Night and Sunday Morning*. Dixon compares Sillitoe's picaresque elitism to Fowles's alleged intellectual elitism.

DITSKY, JOHN. "The Watch and Chain of Henry James." *University of Windsor Review*, 6 (Fall 1970), 91–101. An uncommonly perceptive review article which sees *The French Lieutenant's Woman* and Saul Bellow's *Mr. Sammler's Planet* as humanly responsible fiction in the time-conscious Henry James tradition.

EDDINS, DWIGHT. "John Fowles: Existence as Authorship." *Contemporary Literature*, 17 (Spring 1976), 204–22. Incisively analyzes the relationship between living an existentially authentic life and creating existentially authentic fiction, using a partly archetypal approach and chiding William J. Palmer for treating the subject inadequately in his study of Fowles. Deals with Fowles's first three novels only.

EVARTS, PRESCOTT, JR. "Fowles' *The French Lieutenant's Woman* as Tragedy." *Critique*, 13 (1972), 57–69. Grasps far afield to treat the novel as Mannerist tragedy. Marginally coherent.

———. "John Fowles: A Checklist." *Critique*, 13 (1972), 105–7. An early Fowles checklist.

FRANKLYN, A. FREDRIC. "The Hand in the Fist (A Study of William Wyler's *The Collector*)." *Trace*, 60 (Spring 1966), 22–27, 101–7. Deals only with Wyler's film—not with the novel.

FLEISHMAN, AVROM. "*The Magus* of the Wizard of the West." *Journal of Modern Literature*, 5 (April 1976), 297–314. A clear and intelligent analysis of ritual and symbol in *The Magus*, with pertinent references to Fowles's views set forth in *The Aristos*.

GARDNER, JOHN. "Moral Fiction." *Saturday Review*, 1 April 1978, pp. 30–33. A general discussion of how much contemporary authors display, or fail to display, attitudes of moral responsibility toward their fiction. Cites *Daniel Martin* as embodying the compassion and will of a morally responsible author.

GROSSKURTH, PHYLLIS. *"The French Lieutenant's Woman." Victorian Studies*, 16 (September 1972), 130–31. An unfortunate allegation that Fowles drew his book from an obscure Victorian novella he had never even heard of.

HIETT, CONSTANCE B. *"Eliduc* Revisited: John Fowles and Marie de France." *English Studies in Canada*, 3 (Fall 1977), 351–58. Centers upon the medieval Celtic romance in *The Ebony Tower*.

KANE, PATRICIA. "The Fallen Woman as Free-thinker in *The French Lieutenant's Woman* and *The Scarlet Letter." Notes on Contemporary Literature*, 2 (January 1972), 8–10. An unwarranted feminist assumption that male writers share the social prejudices they portray in fiction.

KAPLAN, FRED. "Victorian Modernists: Fowles and Nabokov." *The Journal of Narrative Technique*, 3 (May 1973), 108–20. Treats *The French Lieutenant's Woman* and Nabokov's *Ada* as centrally concerned with the relationship of fiction to fact. Thesis lacks support.

KARL, FREDERICK R. *A Reader's Guide to the Contemporary English Novel*. Rev. ed. New York: Farrar, Straus and Giroux, 1972. Mentions Fowles admiringly on pp. 323, 326, 342, 344, 355–60. Karl is a reliable and proven authority.

KENNEDY, ALAN. "John Fowles's Sense of an Ending." In *The Protean Self: Dramatic Action in Contemporary Fiction*. New York: Columbia University Press, 1974. Pp. 251–60. Wonders at the complexity of *The Magus* and puts *The French Lieutenant's Woman* into a thesis about dramatic action.

LAUGHLIN, ROSEMARY M. "Faces of Power in the Novels of John Fowles." *Critique*, 13 (1972), 71–88. Discusses Fowles's first three novels as being centrally concerned with the power which people wield over others. Makes some perceptive observations while trying to support a weak thesis.

MAGALANER, MARVIN. "The Fool's Journey: John Fowles's *The Magus* (1966)." In *Old Lines, New Forces: Essays on the Contemporary British Novel, 1960–1976*, edited by Robert K. Morris, pp. 81–92. Cranbury, New York: Associated University Presses, 1976. An intelligent analysis of the novel's Tarot symbolism which wisely allows room for multiple interpretations.

MATHEWS, JAMES W. "Fowles's Artistic Freedom: Another Stone from James's House." *Notes on Contemporary Literature*, 4 (March 1974), 2–4. Notes parallels between James's and Fowles's attitudes toward their characters' reality.

McDOWELL, F. P. W. "Recent British Fiction: Some Established Writers." *Contemporary Literature*, 11 (Summer 1970), 401–31. Ranks *The French Lieutenant's Woman* above all other British fiction from late 1967 through autumn 1969, and, on pp. 428–31, provides an excellent reading of the novel. Is especially astute in observing that Fowles's use of authorial intrusions illustrates principles set forth by Wayne C. Booth in *The Rhetoric of Fiction.*

MCGREGOR, BARBARA R. "Existentialism in *The French Lieutenant's Woman.*" *RE: Artes Liberales*, 1, no. 2 (1975), 39–46. Discusses existentialist qualities of the characters and their situations.

MELLORS, JOHN. "Collectors and Creators: The Novels of John Fowles." *London Magazine*, 14, no. 6 (1975), 65–72. A bit too cleverly, divides all Fowles characters into collectors and creators; misclassifies Fowles himself as a collector.

MYERS, KAREN MAGEE. "John Fowles: An Annotated Bibliography, 1963–1976." *Bulletin of Bibliography*, 32 (July–September 1976), 162–69. Helpful, but contains troublesome errors. Useful for its information about translations of Fowles's books.

OLSHEN, BARRY N. *John Fowles.* New York: Frederick Ungar, 1978. The first judicious book-length study published about Fowles and his works. Complete through *Daniel Martin.*

———, and Olshen, Toni. *John Fowles: A Reference Guide.* Boston: G. K. Hall, 1980. A comprehensive, annotated bibliography of works by and about Fowles, with an introduction which traces his career through 1978.

PALMER, WILLIAM J. *The Fiction of John Fowles.* Columbia: University of Missouri Press, 1974. A lightly documented discussion of existentialism and literary influence in Fowles's first three novels.

PRESLEY, DELMA E. "The Quest of the Bourgeois Hero: An Approach to Fowles's *The Magus.*" *Journal of Popular Culture*, 6 (Fall 1972), 394–98. Discusses sociological aspects of the hero's situation, proceeding upon a mistranslation of Fowles's initial DeSade epigram.

RACKHAM, JEFF. "John Fowles: The Existential Labyrinth." *Critique*, 13 (1972), 89–103. A rather thin discussion of Fowles's first three novels.

RANKIN, ELIZABETH D. "Cryptic Coloration in *The French Lieutenant's Woman.*" *The Journal of Narrative Technique*, 3 (September 1973), 193–207. A sensible and perceptive reading of the novel, calling the narrator's protests about his characters' autonomy a sort of "cryptic coloration" to conform to contemporary ideas of freedom.

ROSE, GILBERT J. "*The French Lieutenant's Woman:* The Unconscious Significance of a Novel to Its Author." *American Imago*, 29 (Summer 1972), 165–76. A penetrating analysis of the parent-child relationship, sexuality, and the unconscious mind behind Fowles's creation of the novel. A literary psychoanalysis written by a professor of clinical psychiatry at Yale. Interesting to Fowles, who mentions this article prominently in "Hardy and the Hag."

RUBENSTEIN, ROBERTA. "Myth, Mystery, and Irony: John Fowles's *The Magus.*" *Contemporary Literature*, 16 (Summer 1975), 328–39. Critically evaluates the novel, considering early reviews, *The Aristos*, and Fowles's fiction through *The Ebony Tower.*

SCHOLES, ROBERT. "The Illiberal Imagination." *New Literary History*, 4 (Spring 1973), 521–40. Mentions Fowles only to illustrate the development of the modern literary imagination from liberalism through existentialism into structuralism. One would do well to read this brilliant landmark in history-of-ideas criticism.

————. "The Orgastic Fiction of John Fowles." *The Hollins Critic*, 6 (December 1969), 1–12. Misrepresented in two published bibliographies as "Orgiastic," Scholes's enlightened article likens Fowles's technique of suspense to delay of orgasm. Fowles admires Scholes as one of the few critics who seem to see him as he sees himself.

TATHAM, MICHAEL. "Two Novels: Notes on the Work of John Fowles." *New Blackfriars*, 52 (September 1971), 404–11. A perceptive and interesting analysis of *The French Lieutenant's Woman* from a religious perspective.

WOLFE, PETER. *John Fowles, Magus and Moralist*. Lewisburg, Pa.: Bucknell University Press, 1976. An understanding study of Fowles's first three novels, treating them, however, as more prescriptive than descriptive.

2. Interviews and Biographical Articles

AMORY, MARK. "Tales Out of School." *Sunday Times Magazine*, 22 September 1974, pp. 33–35. One of the best interview features on Fowles. Amory lets Fowles do most of the talking, and the article consequently reveals information from the time of Fowles's childhood to that of his current work.

BAKER, JOHN F. "John Fowles." *Publishers Weekly*, 25 November 1974, pp. 6–7. An article quoting Fowles extensively after an interview with him. Discusses *The Ebony Tower* and mentions Fowles's upcoming visit to New Mexico, a setting he was to include in his next book, *Daniel Martin*.

BOSTON, RICHARD. "John Fowles, Alone But Not Lonely." *New York Times Book Review*, 9 November 1969, pp. 2, 52–53. An especially sensitive biographical article.

CAMPBELL, JAMES. "An Interview with John Fowles." *Contemporary Literature*, 17, no. 4 (1976), 455–69. An extensive, intelligent, and enlightening interview conducted at Fowles's Lyme Regis home on 8 December 1974.

DAVIS, DOUGLAS M. "He Is Like a Lion with Painted Nails." *The National Observer*, 24 January 1966, p. 21. An informative account of a meeting with Fowles. Betrays the atmosphere of a sparring match between Fowles and the interviewer.

GUSSOW, MEL. "Talk with John Fowles." *New York Times Book Review*, 13 November 1977, pp. 3, 84–85. A good biographical article which quotes Fowles about his life and *Daniel Martin*.

HALPERN, DANIEL. "A Sort of Exile in Lyme Regis." *London Magazine,* 10 (March 1971), 34–46. An interview conducted at Fowles's Lyme Regis home. He talks of his solitude, discusses the genesis of his first three novels, and defends the novel over the cinema as "an astounding freedom to choose."

HARTE, BARBARA, and RILEY, CAROLINE, eds. *200 Contemporary Authors.* Detroit: Gale Research Co., 1969. Pp. 117–18. Biographical sketch and description of his first three novels and *The Aristos.* Drawn from previously published sources.

HAUPTFUHRER, FRED. "His Stories are Riddles Wrapped Inside an Enigma Named Fowles." *People,* 7 April 1975, pp. 56–59. A biographical feature which quotes both Fowles and his wife. Undistinguished except for excellent black-and-white photographs of the Fowleses.

HOWARD, MICHAEL S. *Jonathan Cape, Publisher/Herbert Jonathan Cape, G. Wren Howard.* London: Jonathan Cape, 1971. A fiftieth-anniversary commemorative history by the son of cofounder Howard, who, with Cape, established the business in 1921. Contains bits of information about Fowles, Edward Garnett, T. E. Lawrence, Ian Fleming, Ernest Hemingway, Sinclair Lewis, Malcolm Lowry, William Plomer, and Mary Webb.

"John Fowles." *Current Biography,* 38, no. 3 (1977), 11–15. A biographical sketch compiled principally from previously published sources.

MCNAY, MICHAEL. "Into the City's Iron Heart." *Manchester Guardian,* 5 December 1970, p. 8. Feature article on the occasion of Fowles's accepting the W. H. Smith literary award for his latest novel, *The French Lieutenant's Woman.*

MONAGHAN, CHARLES. "Portrait of a Man Reading." *Book World, Chicago Tribune* and *Washington Post,* 4 January 1970, p. 1. A remarkably extensive account of Fowles's readings at various stages of his early development.

NATHAN, PAUL S. "Fowles into Film." *Publishers Weekly,* 4 August 1975, p. 32. Notes Twentieth Century Fox's reselling *The French Lieutenant's Woman* film rights to Paramount in another effort to convert the novel to cinema. Also mentions screenplay plans for "The Ebony Tower." Both motion picture ventures were apparently foredoomed.

NEWQUIST, ROY, ed. "John Fowles." *Counterpoint.* New York: Simon and Schuster, 1964. Pp. 217–25. The most extensive early interview with Fowles, conducted in London, October, 1963, six months after Fowles had quit teaching to devote full time to writing. Focuses upon *The Collector* and the existentialist perspective.

NICHOLS, LEWIS. "Mr. Fowles." *New York Times Book Review,* 30 January 1966, p. 8. Cursory notes on mixed reviews for *The Magus,* Fowles's tentative plans to do the novel's screenplay, his Dorset home, etc.

"No P.L.R. Candidate for St. Marylebone." *Bookseller,* 17 October 1970, pp. 2098–100. Only peripherally devoted to Fowles, whom it mentions as having withdrawn his transitory candidacy in the St. Marylebone district. Fowles had reluctantly agreed to the venture as his duty to the Public Lending Right cause; foreseeing a futile, nine-candidate fiasco, he exercised the better part of valor.

NORTH, DAVID. "Interview with Author John Fowles." *Maclean's*, 14 November 1977, pp. 4, 6, 8. Principally devoted to a discussion of *Daniel Martin*, with mention of *The Ebony Tower*.

ROBINSON, ROBERT. "Giving the Reader a Choice—A Conversation with John Fowles." *The Listener*, 31 October 1974, pp. 584–85. An interview on the BBC's *The Book Programme*, devoted entirely to the newly-published *The Ebony Tower*.

SAGE, LORNA. "John Fowles." *The New Review*, 1 (October 1974), 31–37. An especially good personal profile done after an interview with Fowles. Contains information about his manner, ideas, and career. Three good photographs of Fowles.

STOLLEY, RICHARD B. "The French Lieutenant's Woman's Man." *Life*, 29 May 1970, pp. 55–60. A rather good biographical feature article with excellent black-and-white photographs showing Fowles, Elizabeth, Lyme, the Cobb, and the Dairy.

WAKEMAN, JOHN, ed. "John Fowles." In *World Authors*. New York: H. W. Wilson Co., 1975. Pp. 485–87. Biographical sketch drawn partly from Fowles's own current account as well as from previously published information. Some cursory bibliographical information.

WANSELL, GEOFFREY. "The Writer as a Recluse." *London Times*, 12 May 1971, p. 14. A bit of current biographical data focused upon Fowles's growing popular acclaim, his financial success, and his need for privacy.

3. Reviews of Fowles's Major Books

a. *The Aristos*
Books and Bookmen, 13 (August 1968), 45.
Choice, 2 (March 1965), 16–17.
GRAY, RICHARD A. *Library Journal*, 15 January 1965, p. 252.
HOPE, FRANCIS. *The Observer*, 13 June 1965, p. 27.
MORTIMER, JOHN. *The New Statesman*, 2 July 1965, p. 16.
SCHOLES, ROBERT. *Saturday Review*, 17 October 1970, pp. 36–37.
Time, 20 November 1964, pp. 110–11.
Times Literary Supplement, 8 July 1965, p. 585.

b. *The Collector*
AUCHINCLOSS, EVE. *New York Review of Books*. 14 November 1963, pp. 17–18.
BALLIETT, WHITNEY. *The New Yorker*, 28 September 1963, pp. 192–93.
BROOKE, JOCELYN. *The Listener*, 23 May 1963, p. 883.
BROPHY, BRIGID. *The New Statesman*, 21 June 1963, p. 942.

DAVENPORT, BASIL, *Book of the Month Club News*, September 1963, p. 8.
DAVENPORT, GUY. *National Review*, 5 November 1963, pp. 401–2.
DEBELLIS, JACK. *Sewanee Review*, 72 (Summer 1964), 532.
FULLER, EDMUND. *Chicago Sunday Tribune Magazine of Books*, 28 July 1963, p. 3.
GARDINER, HAROLD C. *America*, 27 July 1963, p. 99.
GENET. *The New Yorker*, 5 November 1966, pp. 162–63.
GRIFFIN, LLOYD. *Library Journal*, 88 (August 1963), 2926.
HALIO, JAY L. *The Southern Review*, 2 (Autumn 1966), 952–66.
HICKS, GRANVILLE. *Saturday Review*, 27 July 1963, pp. 19–20.
MCGUINNESS, FRANK. *London Magazine*, 3 (August 1963), 84–86.
MURRAY, MICHELE. *Commonweal*, 1 November 1963, pp. 172–73.
OCHS, MAXWELL DAVID. *Minnesota Review*, 4 (Spring 1964), 459–61.
PHELPS, ROBERT. *New York Herald Tribune Books*, 28 July 1963, p. 9.
PICKREL, PAUL. *Harper's Magazine*, 227 (August 1963), 95–96.
PRESCOTT, ORVILLE. *New York Times*, 24 July 1963, p. 29.
PRYCE-JONES, ALAN. *New York Times Book Review*, 28 July 1963, pp. 4, 12.
RENEK, MORRIS. *The Nation*, 23 November 1963, pp. 352–53.
SALE, ROGER. *Hudson Review*, 16 (Winter 1963–1964), 604.
SCHICKEL, RICHARD. *Show*, 3 (August 1963), 40.
Time, 2 August 1963, p. 68.
Times Literary Supplement, 17 May 1963, p. 353.
Times Weekly Review, 30 May 1963, p. 13.
TRACY, HONOR. *The New Republic*, 3 August 1963, pp. 20–21.
VANDERBILT, GLORIA. *Cosmopolitan*, 155 (July 1963), 26.
Virginia Quarterly Review, 39 (Autumn 1963), cxx.
WOOD, FREDERICK T. *English Studies*, 45 (June 1964), 260–63.

c. *Daniel Martin*
BURGESS, ANTHONY. *The Irish Press*, 13 October 1977.
CAPLAN, LINCOLN. *The Boston Phoenix*, 4 April 1978, sec. 3, p. 10.
DEFEO, RONALD. *National Review*, 3 March 1978, pp. 288–89.
DONOGHUE, DENIS. *New York Review of Books*, 8 December 1977, pp. 45–46.
DOWNING, MARGARET. *Dallas Times Herald*, 11 September 1977, sec. E, p. 4.
GARDNER, JOHN. *Saturday Review*, 1 October 1977, pp. 22–24.
GRAY, PAUL. *Time*, 12 September 1977, p. 75.
LEHMANN-HAUPT, CHRISTOPHER. *New York Times*, 13 September 1977, p. 29.
MASON, MICHAEL. *Times Literary Supplement*, 7 October 1977, p. 1135.
MCSWEENEY, KERRY. *Critical Quarterly*, 20 (Winter 1978), 31–38.
ᴾRITCHARD, WILLIAM H. *New York Times Book Review*, 25 September 1977, pp. 1, 42.

RUBENSTEIN, ROBERTA. *The Progressive*, 41 (November 1977), 55–56.

d. *The Ebony Tower*
BAILY, PAUL. *The Observer*, 6 October 1974, p. 30.
BRYANT, RENE KUHN. *National Review*, 17 January 1975, pp. 51–53.
The Economist, 30 November 1974, p. 10.
FABER, RODERICK M. *Village Voice*, 14 November 1974, p. 47.
HILL, WILLIAM B. *Best Sellers*, 15 December 1974, p. 421.
HIRSCH, FOSTER. *America*, 11 January 1975, pp. 18–19.
Kirkus Reviews, 1 September 1974, p. 959.
LEHMANN-HAUPT, CHRISTOPHER. *New York Times*, 4 November 1974, p. 35.
Library Journal, 1 October 1974, p. 2499.
MORRIS, ROBERT K. *The Nation*, 13 September 1975, pp. 214–15.
MORROW, LANCE. *Time*, 2 December 1974, pp. 108, K10.
Newsweek, 25 November 1974, pp. 120, 123.
New Yorker, 23 December 1974, pp. 83–84.
PRINCE, PETER. *The New Statesman*, 11 October 1974, p. 513.
Publishers' Weekly, 16 September 1974, p. 54.
SOLOTAROFF, THEODORE. *New York Times Book Review*, 10 November 1974, pp. 2–3, 20.
WEEKS, EDWARD. *Atlantic*, 234 (December 1974), 126.

e. *The French Lieutenant's Woman*
Antioch Review, 29 (Winter 1969–1970), 587–88.
BELL, PEARL K. *The New Leader*, 5 January 1970, pp. 19–20.
CAPITANCHIK, M. *Spectator*, 14 June 1969, p. 788.
CHASE, EDWARD T. *The New Republic*, 15 November 1969, pp. 23–24.
DAVENPORT, GUY. *National Review*, 2 December 1969, pp. 1223–26.
EDWARDS, LEE R. *The Massachusetts Review*, 11 (Summer 1970), 604–8.
FULLER, EDMUND. *The Wall Street Journal*, 19 November 1969, p. 22.
GORDON, JAN B. *The Southern Review*, 9 (Winter 1973), 222–27.
GRANT, ANNETTE. *The Nation*, 15 December 1969, pp. 667–68.
GRAY, PAUL EDWARD. *The Yale Review*, 59 (Spring, 1970), 430–32.
HAMILTON, IAN. *The Listener*, 3 July 1969, p. 24.
LEHMANN-HAUPT, CHRISTOPHER. *New York Times*, 10 November 1969, p. 45.
McDOWELL, FREDERICK P. W. *Contemporary Literature*, 11 (Summer 1970), 401–31.
OATES, JOYCE CAROL. *Book World, Chicago Tribune and Washington Post*, 2 November 1969, pp. 1, 3.
PRICE, JAMES. *The New Statesman*, 13 June 1969, p. 850.
RICKS, CHRISTOPHER. *New York Review of Books*, 12 February 1970, pp. 22–24.
SALE, ROGER. *Hudson Review*, 22 (Winter 1969–1970), 710–12.

SCHICKEL, RICHARD. *Harper's Magazine,* 239 (December 1969), 146.
SCOTT-KILVERT, IAN. *British Book News,* June 1971, pp. 425–30.
SOKOLOV, RAYMOND A. *Newsweek,* 10 November 1969, pp. 118–20.
Time, 7 November 1969, p. 108.
Times Literary Supplement, 12 June 1969, p. 629.
Virginia Quarterly Review, 46 (Spring 1970), XL.
WATT, IAN. *New York Times Book Review,* 9 November 1969., pp. 1, 74–75.
WEEKS, EDWARD. *Atlantic Monthly,* 225 (January 1970), 98–99.
WOLFE, PETER. *Saturday Review,* 22 November 1969, p. 85.

f. *The Magus*
BERGONZI, BERNARD. *New York Review of Books,* 17 March 1966, p. 20.
Best Sellers, 1 April 1973, p. 22.
Books and Bookmen, 13 (August 1968), 46.
Booklist, 1 February 1966, p. 519.
BURGESS, ANTHONY. *The Listener,* 5 May 1966, p. 659.
BYROM, BILL. *The Spectator,* 6 May 1966, p. 574.
Choice, 3 (September 1966), 518–19.
CULLIGAN, GLENDY. *The Reporter,* 24 February 1966, pp. 56–58.
DAVENPORT, G. *National Review,* 12 July 1966, p. 696.
DONAHUE, H. E. F. *Holiday,* 39 (February 1966), 124, 126–27.
EPSTEIN, JOSEPH. *The New Republic,* 19 February 1966, pp. 26–29.
FLEISCHER, LEONORE. *Publisher's Weekly,* 28 November 1966, p. 62.
FREMONT-SMITH, ELIOT. *New York Times,* 17 January 1966, p. 45.
GRIFFIN, LLOYD W. *Library Journal,* 15 December 1965, p. 5414.
LINDROTH, JAMES R. *America,* 12 February 1966, p. 234.
LYNCH, WILLIAM J. *Best Sellers,* 15 January 1966, pp. 402–3.
MOORE, BRIAN. *New York Herald Tribune Book Week,* 9 January 1966, pp. 4, 12.
MORTIMER, PENELOPE. *The New Statesman,* 6 May 1966, p. 659.
MUDRICK, MARVIN. *Hudson Review,* 19 (Summer 1966), 305–18.
MULVEY, CHRISTOPHER E. *Commonweal,* 1 April 1966, pp. 60–61.
Newsweek, 17 January 1966, p. 87.
Newsweek, 19 December 1966, p. 118.
The New Yorker, 16 April 1966, pp. 198–99.
Publisher's Weekly, 15 July 1968, p. 59.
SAMSTAG, NICHOLAS. *Saturday Review,* 15 January 1966, p. 40.
SCOTT, J. D. *New York Times Book Review,* 9 January 1966, pp. 4–5.
SCOTT-KILVERT, IAN. *British Book News,* 322 (June 1967), 409–14.
SHUTTLEWORTH, MARTIN. *Punch,* 4 May 1966, p. 668.
Time, 14 January 1966, pp. 92–93.
Times Literary Supplement, 5 May 1966, p. 381.
WILSON, ANGUS. *The Observer,* 1 May 1966, p. 27; reprint, *Critic,* 25 (August 1966), 50–51.

g. *Poems*
Booklist, 15 September 1973, p. 77
Kirkus Reviews, 15 March 1973, p. 353.
Library Journal, 1 May 1973, p. 1493.
PERLMAN, ANNE S. *San Francisco Chronicle,* 4 January 1974.
WOLFE, PETER. *Contemporary Poetry,* 1 (1973), 69–72.

Index